Embracing
Schizophrenia

My Story of Struggle, Strength, Resilience and Hope

Samantha Mercanti

The lotus is a sacred plant with deep meaning, sometimes seen as a symbol of awakening. Every morning the flower re-blooms from the murky water. The lotus reminds me that every day you can re-emerge beautifully from the darkness into the sunlight.

Published by Samantha Mercanti
Hamilton, Ontario, Canada
SamanthaMercanti.com/contact-me/

ISBN: 978-1-7777136-0-7

Edited by Donna L. Dawson, CPE
Page layout by Sheila M. Mahoney
Cover design by Tania Paskulin
Author photo by Amanda DeMelo

I would like to dedicate this book to my three nieces and two nephews. The five of you have brought me so much joy and peace and love and have made my journey so much more amazing just by being in my life. I am grateful every single day for each and every one of you.

Contents

Foreword

Serious mental illness is confusing for those witnessing their loved ones going through it and even more confusing for those experiencing it. Anyone wanting to appreciate what serious mental illness is like and what it takes to begin a path to recovery needs to read this book. It is filled with heartwarming commentaries and narratives from family members and friends. Samantha's story will inspire and invigorate you to find the strength to believe in yourself and to keep healing yourself with the support of your loved ones and your care team.

Samantha reveals her emotional pain, perceptual disturbances and confusion so you can understand what psychosis is like for her and countless others who may not be in a position to give voice to their experiences. In her recounting, she has shown us how to pick up the pieces and gradually rebuild and transform one life into something whole, healthy and new. She will teach you how she opened herself to support from loved ones and friends and some of the healing solutions that helped her care for herself.

I can only say how privileged and proud I feel to play a small part in promoting this book, which will touch many people's lives. Samantha shows us how to find the courage and resilience to come back from serious mental illness to find joy and meaning in life.

Suzanne Archie, MD, FRCPC
Professor, Department of Psychiatry
and Behavioural Neurosciences
McMaster University

Introduction.
Life Is Hard,
But Full of Lessons

Perfection is a little overrated.

Life is hard. Everyone tells you life is a journey, a road, a path. What they forget to tell you is that life is far from easy and far from perfect. What we also need to know is that there will be lessons on this journey. There will be good lessons but most importantly there will be difficult lessons. And to grow and become better we need to learn from these lessons – the good and the bad. I truly believe that life will only make sense if we learn from the lessons it teaches.

Everyone takes a unique path in their life and we all need to realize that the path we take is the right path for us, even if it might not seem like it sometimes. The road you travelled was the path you were supposed to take. It took me years to figure this out but once I realized it, I started to really understand it and accept that what happened to me was supposed to happen. I never took a wrong turn; I never made the wrong choice. I always took the right turn to bring me to where I am now.

When I was younger, I had a detailed life plan and I knew exactly where I was going and how I would get there. At least I thought I did. I knew that I would go to the best university, study every waking hour to get the best grades and become a doctor – a neurosurgeon, to be exact. I was smart and I knew I could do it. After medical school, I would marry the man of my dreams, my soul mate! I knew exactly who he was and I loved him deeply. We would love each other until our last breath.

We would have "2.5" children, and the kids would ask us for a dog. At first we would say no but then we would give in and get them a puppy, which would live forever. Our children would love life just like we did. They would have faith, but not so much faith that they became judgemental. They would grow up and be successful in life, just like my husband and I. They would have the values we raised them to have. Life would be great for them and for their kids and so on.

Does anyone honestly think this is the way life works? That all our plans and all our hopes and dreams actually come true? That our lives will end up like a perfect fairy tale, played out like a movie? I did. I honestly thought my life would turn out this way. I am not sure whether society creates the expectation that we can have everything – the perfect life, the perfect family, the perfect fairy tale – or whether it is we who hold ourselves to a standard of perfection. I feel a little like I was deceived by everyone around me, and maybe even by myself. I actually thought the fairy tale would come true.

Do you want to know what really happened?

My life turned out very different from what I thought would happen. The fairy tale definitely did not come true. If only I had burned that idea years ago and faced reality.

Though my journey might not sound as perfect as that fairy tale, to me it is better. It is what God and the universe wanted for me. My journey was the path I was supposed to take, and my illness, as scary and difficult as it was, has been the greatest life lesson I have received. My illness and what I went through was a lesson I needed.

I left the fairy tale behind in the mind of that guileless teenager, where it will stay; I don't want it anymore. It was too easy, too perfect. What I wanted and what I needed were two very different things back then.

I needed life lessons. What I have learned is that if you do not learn from the lessons you're given and if you do not continue to want to learn from them, you will not truly understand your purpose in this world or what the universe has planned for you or wants you to accomplish.

The story of my life is about some good days and some bad days, good hours and bad hours, good moments and bad moments.

And don't get me wrong: even with those bad times, I absolutely love my life.

Some moments are amazing, breathtaking and beautiful! Sometimes I can't believe the universe wants to show me this beauty. And then sometimes, the universe can be absolutely awful to me. I guess this is what it is to live a life with a mental illness.

Or maybe this is just what it means to live a life. I speak to a lot of people who have never been diagnosed with a mental illness, and they often tell me they struggle and are not one hundred percent happy. Everyone has good days and bad days, good moments and bad moments.

One thing I have learned talking to people about mental illness is that validating others' thoughts and feelings is the best thing to do. Every person's feelings matter, no matter how small or how large the issue is. Every emotion matters, as long as it is respectful and non-discriminatory. We need to remember that we all matter. You will see comments from my family and friends throughout this book, telling their side of my story. This story is about me, but everyone around me matters in my story.

Trying to learn how to live life with a mental illness is not easy, trust me; it took me probably fifteen years to truly figure out my illness. And I keep learning new things about myself and my illness every day.

Navigating our minds while trying to maintain some type of control in a world you have no control over can be very difficult. I don't think "very difficult" can even really describe what I go through daily. It is something I cannot explain, and to be honest I don't really like to focus on how I feel daily. I have learned that some days I will feel a certain way. And I know that I will manage it, I will get through the day, validate my feelings, feel what I feel and move on.

In this book, I try to explain a little bit of my story, what I go through, what my family goes through, what I have learned and what life has taught me. I wish what I went through upon no one. I wish and hope that not one person ever has to experience what I have experienced. I know people will, but one of the many reasons I am so open about my experience is that I don't want anyone to go through what I went through. My illness broke me – to pieces, to nothing. But my illness also brought me back into this world with a better mindset and a stronger character.

A long time ago I chose to focus on the positive parts of my illness and my life. I decided that I was not going to let this world defeat me. I knew from the beginning of my illness that I was going to beat it, and if I died trying, so be it. I know you can overcome mental illness because I did it.

And I would die trying to enable every single person with a mental illness to overcome it. I will continue to push for rights for everyone with mental illness, and I will continue until the day I leave this earth.

I believe one of the reasons my recovery has been so successful is that I told myself I will fight.

I will fight every second of every day for myself, and I will never, ever give up on myself.

My illness taught me so much about life, and the times when I was at my lowest points were the times I learned the most about myself and my journey in this world. I wish everyone could see how much they are learning in their darkest moments. I have seen the most beautiful parts of life and the most broken parts of life. Even in the most broken times, there is an amazing beauty, and I wish everyone could see that because I found it in my broken self.

I love that I am able to share my story. I think that's one reason my recovery has been so successful. From the very beginning of my recovery I have been open about my experience with mental illness. And don't get me wrong – my recovery is far from perfect, and I mean very, very far from perfect. But I am able to live a pretty good life and manage my illness. And remember, sometimes "perfect" is not all it's cracked up to be. I think it's a little overrated.

I do talk openly to everyone about my mental health, and theirs, even complete strangers. I will talk to people I meet at a store or anywhere I am. I talk about mental health whenever I have a minute of anyone's time. And people have shared so many stories with me! They tell me about their brother, their aunt, their cousin, their friend, their friend's friend, their daughter or son, their grandparent. I have heard so many stories about people living with mental illness or being connected to someone who has a mental illness.

It used to be that people would say to me they did not know anyone with a mental illness. At first, I always wanted to laugh (I did not, of course) because I knew that they probably knew lots of people with a mental illness. They might not have realized it, but they definitely knew someone with a mental illness.

We are all affected by mental illness whether we realize it or not. We are all part of everyone's mental illness and mental health, and we all need to realize this and figure out ways to make our society and community stronger by making people with mental illness stronger.

When I share my story, all I want people to know is that number one, you can get through it and you are going to be okay. With strength, hope, faith, determination and of course a little hard work, balance and self-examination, you can thrive, be successful in life and understand that you are entitled to live a good and decent life even if you have a mental illness.

It may not be perfect, but it is possible.

My journey is unique to me. Each and every person with a mental illness will have a unique journey and a unique recovery. I want every person to know they can recover and manage their illness.

I also want people to know that your experience with whatever mental illness you have will, if you let it, be the greatest lesson of your life. It will teach you strength and compassion and it will give you a different and better perspective on life. But only if you let it.

I knew that this illness was not going to be the end of my story, it was going to be the beginning.

You will read about what I learned throughout this book, and what my family learned. Remember, you, your friend, your family member or that person sitting next to you somewhere at some time may have a mental illness or may have been touched by mental illness. Tell yourself, or that other person: Be kind to yourself. Support yourself and remind yourself to never, ever forget the strength you have inside. Remind yourself to never give up, to fight, to be open if you're ready. Love yourself. Understand that life is going to be difficult at times, but never give up on your yourself.

Read this book and realize that you can manage your illness, just like I did. And if you are not yet at the point where you are ready to manage your illness, know that I believe you can get there. It won't be easy, it won't be perfect, but successful recovery is possible.

I feel like we sometimes focus too much on the illness and forget about the recovery. I truly believe people can recover and live amazing lives with mental illness and I am living proof it can be done.

So, this is my story. You might agree with what I say or not. It's fine if you don't always agree with me. But I know that what I learned about life has changed me forever. My story made me a better person, it made me want to always strive to be a better person, and I hope by reading this you can learn something about life, about mental illness or about your path or journey. You may even find a little happiness, joy and peace in my words.

Remember, if you are struggling with mental illness, stay strong, stay focused and understand that you can find peace in all the madness.

If you ever think you're not capable of recovering, your mind is deceiving you. Forget about the illness and focus on the recovery. Remember your strength. It's there in you and it will always be there.

I hope you find what I found, because I would not trade it for anything in this world. If you threw money at me, or power to change the path I took, I would respectfully decline. I would not think of changing the path I took. I was given a gift by God and the universe and I would not give this gift up for anything. It was a lesson for me. It was a difficult lesson, but it was something that had to be learned, because it changed my perspective on life and my purpose in it.

If I could do it all over again, I would pick the path I took over my perfect fairy tale – every time.

Chapter 1.
The Beginnings

Different might actually be better.

I had no idea what was happening to me at fifteen years old. I was very angry at the world and I did not understand my feelings. I remember slamming my hands onto my bed because I was so mad. I felt so much hate and anger at everyone around me. I wanted to die in those moments. I did not want this anger. But something in me kept me going, something kept me on this earth and fighting. Honestly, I am not one hundred percent sure why I kept fighting, why I stayed. It might have been God, or it might have been my own will knowing that I would somehow get through this pain and suffering.

I don't know why I was so angry. I did endure some traumatic experiences when I was young and vulnerable, in my childhood and when I was a teenager. I talk to my therapist about these events but I may never be ready to share them. I was taken advantage of because of my innocence, and my innocence was taken from me. Part of my anger was because of those experiences. I thought I had forgiven everyone involved a long time ago, but forgiveness and healing are not linear. I don't think those people realize even to this day how much those experiences affected me and my wellbeing, and that they may have affected my mental health and contributed to my spiralling out of control.

I have recovered from my past. I have had to forgive many people in my life. Years ago, I chose to move on from my past and the negative experiences from that time and that is the last I will speak of that part of my life. I know the people involved will have to face God one day, and God will judge them for what they did to me.

What was I like as a kid? My eldest sister says that growing up, I was always smiling and very happy. My middle sister agrees – happy and outgoing. My eldest sister's husband says, "When I first met Samantha, she was a smart, energetic, and feisty teenager. We hit it off quickly, as we both liked to debate what was going on in the world, and our taste in music was pretty similar, especially when it came to grunge. I really believe my initial relationship with Samantha truly helped me fit in to the Mercanti family, and I will forever be grateful for that."

School was my happy place. I was a remarkable student. My goal was to get good grades and go to a university far away from my parents. I was a typical teenager at first. I wanted to escape my parents' grasp and live independently very far from them.

My mind was so lost sometimes when I was in high school. I was not able to understand reality and my place in it. I had no idea what was going on in my mind. I did not understand what was happening to me, why I was so angry at the world or why I was feeling the emotions I felt.

Eventually, after my diagnosis, I realized I had had a mental illness when I was fifteen – or even earlier – but no one knew. Or maybe they did not want to talk about it or to help me. There were many times between the age of ten and twenty when I called indirectly for help, hoping someone would save me. No one answered.

I have since learned that some people saw the signs. My mother said that seeing me smoking outside my school was probably the first time she thought something might be wrong. After all, I was the reason my dad had quit smoking. When I was in grade 12, my mom noticed a few more things, like I was not spending as much time with friends and not enjoying dance as much as I had before. But, she thought, it was just the usual teenage moods.

With my good grades and intense studying, I was accepted into a science program at an amazing university in Eastern Ontario, one of the top schools in Canada, and I started my journey to my perfect fairy tale life. I moved into residence. I was scared, but I knew my goal: study all the time, do not go out a lot, do not drink, prepare for the Medical College Admission Test and then attend medical school. It was happening! I was finally on my way.

Was I lost? Maybe. But I was growing up. I was developing, becoming an adult, and I believe everyone developing from a teenager into an adult is a little lost and broken sometimes.

Little did I know that my journey was about to change, and change drastically.

It was close to the end of my first year of university. Exams were on the horizon. I thought all

I had to do was study and ace these exams, and I would have a pretty decent average. So that's what I did. The night before the week of my first exams, my roommates ordered food for me for dinner. I started eating in the common room, where we gathered to watch television, but I felt like everyone was looking at me.

So I went to my room, alone, with my food. I was eating, and then it happened. I don't know if drugs were put into my food. Looking back, I do believe I may have been drugged, but to this day I do not know what happened. If I was drugged, whoever did it was very smart and knew everyone would think I was crazy and no one would believe me. I do not know if I had a seizure after I ate or if my mind was playing tricks on me, but I fell back onto my bed and blacked out. I think I may have slept for about a day and a half. I had no idea where I was or what was going on.

When I woke, I continued studying and because I could not think properly I stayed up and in my room for ten days straight. I heard people yelling outside my door and window but was told it was all in my head. My mom sent me a care package, so I lived off that during those days. I wrote all my exams in a complete haze. I had no idea where I was or what to do or what was happening to me.

I definitely needed help so I called and called people I knew, but no one wanted anything to do with me. No one answered my phone calls.

I died in those hours. One day changed the course of my entire life. It was as if in that moment I had lost everything without knowing I had lost it. In those moments, some part of me knew I was never going to be the same.

I asked my parents to pick me up at university. My aunt and uncle came to take me home because my parents were moving house that day. I sat quietly in the car, not truly knowing where I was, who I was or what was going on. I sat there thinking or maybe not thinking. I cannot remember anything of that time except just gazing out the car window.

I may have been relieved to be home; I do not really remember. My parents knew something was wrong, and I did too, but I could not speak about it.

Others around me knew something was wrong too. A close friend describes that time:

I had not seen my friends since Christmas and wanted to just spend the summer with them. When we met, I was shocked to see the noticeable change in Samantha. She was physically withdrawn, with tired eyes and dark circles. She was quiet – not the same

Sam I remembered from just a year before. She started to talk about her experience away at school. I tried to follow what she was saying, but I could not. The stories did not make sense to me and I remember trying to ask questions to clarify but met with frustration because I did not understand. I just sat and listened and after the night was done, went home. I found throughout the summer that this was not a one-off. All my interactions with Samantha ended in the same way. I was confused and scared.

I remember that I would hear my friends and family say things they didn't actually say. I would hear their voices say something completely different. That could be why communicating became so difficult for me, which could be why when I spoke no one really understood what I was saying – I heard them say absolutely nothing they were actually saying and I answered questions based on what I heard their voices say to me.

My aunt knew something was wrong too:

As we pulled up into the driveway we saw Samantha sitting outside on the concrete ledge. We exited the car and were walking up toward the front door and as we walked up to her we all said hello but she didn't respond. I proceeded to ask about school and she didn't respond, and this is when I realized that Samantha didn't seem to be listening to me or even acknowledge my presence, our presence.

The very first thought that came to mind was sadness as I felt something was up but of course didn't know what. The first thing I thought of was, could it be drugs? At the same time I thought to myself, no, Samantha wouldn't go down that road, because she was such a bright student...I didn't want to cross the line and ask anyone what was going on, even though I felt deep concern and sadness, because I felt that if the family wanted to share what was going on they would have.

My brother-in-law observed,

The first time I suspected something wasn't right was at the dinner table during one of our weekly Sunday dinners at my in laws'. We were all sitting around the table, eating Samantha's mom's amazing food, talking about the week and enjoying each other's company. Suddenly, out of the corner of my eye, I thought I saw Samantha giggle to herself. It was a bit strange, I thought, but I didn't really think too much of it. It happened again, and again, and then I was sure I saw her mumble some words to herself. At this point, I was now watching around the table to see if anyone else noticed. No one seemed to, or didn't want to notice. I chose not to say anything, even to my wife.

The following Sunday it happened again. Giggles and mumbling. This time, it was more obvious. Again, I looked around the table to see if anyone else was seeing it, and this time I was sure that other people were seeing it, but no one said anything. To this day, I believe that it was just more comfortable for everyone to say nothing. I guess that was how families treated a suspicion of mental illness before. Pretend nothing is wrong, turn a blind eye, and pray that it will stop.

I knew, when I was looking out that car window on my way home from my first year of university, that my life would never ever be the same. In one day, all my dreams and all my goals in life disappeared. But I didn't know what was happening

Embracing Schizophrenia

and I don't think I realized how difficult my life was going to become.

The world broke me that day in my dorm room. I did try to report what happened to me to security at my school. I told the person the whole story, then the person asked me, are you really sure you want to report this? And I hesitated and said, well maybe no. And we left it at that.

Imagine being twenty and knowing that everything you dreamed of and everything you thought your life would be, was gone. My life was never going to be what I thought it would be. I knew that my path was going to change.

Life is hard. Period. Now I understood this. Maybe I would survive, maybe I would not. That was up to me. My goals and dreams and life would be different from this point forward. But on the other end of it all, when I recovered, I understood that different might actually be better.

Chapter 2.
Hearing Voices

A little humour in all
the hell helps a lot.

"I'm hearing things." I uttered these words to my parents while sitting on their pink couch watching TV. That was not something they were expecting to hear but they did know something was wrong.

I was not really scared, yet I was not okay either. It was like I was in this world, but somehow not in this world. It's hard to explain. If someone came up to me, I would be able to talk to them, but at the same time I had no sense of reality. I was there but not truly there. I could answer questions without having any idea what I was being asked, and then I could not remember what was asked of me.

Onto the Christian counsellors. Why Christian counsellors? They were the only people I would talk to and trust. I did not want to go to a hospital or psychiatrist because I was afraid of being locked up in an institution – and because I was paranoid. I was literally scared of everything. People around me might have been scared of me, but I was scared of the world and I didn't know why. All I wanted in my mind was complete and utter peace, yet I knew that state was very, very far away.

My father explains:

I went to see and speak to the priest at our church. Father told me that Samantha may have a mental illness called schizophrenia. I had hardly heard of the term. Because I was on the board of a hospital, I spoke to some doctors who were on the board about her situation. They recommended a doctor at the hospital. I met with him and spoke to my wife about him. We set up an appointment for Samantha to see him. At first she did not want to go, but then she did. But she did not want to go back to him – she was scared of a psychiatrist...

I got her an appointment to see...two great Christian counsellors, but they told us that what was going on was beyond what they could understand, and recommended another Christian...

These two Christian places did not do anything to help your condition.

I thought the Christian counsellors were great. I liked them, mostly because they were not psychiatrists, but they had no idea what was happening to me or what to do. Although I remember that there were two counsellors, I thought that perhaps one had been a figment of my imagination. I did ask my parents years later if he was real.

The counsellors told my parents my illness was way over their heads; they recommended I see someone like a psychiatrist.

Eventually it seemed like no one wanted anything to do with me anymore, except my parents. I guess I was too crazy for everyone. I just wish people could have understood that all I might have needed was someone to talk to, even if I did not know what I was saying or what I was doing in this world.

And here comes the "I wish I was in this world" feeling, because again, I would talk to my parents and counsellors, I would tell them how I was feeling, yet I was not there; I was somewhere else. If I was there, I would have continued to talk to the Christian counsellors because in some ways I feel like there was something the universe was trying to tell me.

I still refused to see a psychiatrist – that was bad mistake number one. I did try a psychologist, but the paranoia got the best of me. I thought a psychologist was way too close to a psychiatrist, so I refused to see the psychologist after one visit.

And onto...bad decision number two! I went back to school in Eastern Ontario for second year, and let me tell you, that was a big mistake. I was absolutely all over the place. And yet, I passed all my courses. How, you ask? I have absolutely no idea. Again, I was not in this world, yet I was able to pass my second year of study for a chemistry degree.

Sometimes I would run outside from my room and sprint across campus because I felt I was going mad. I was going completely and utterly mad. No one wanted to help me or see if I needed help. I cried and cried, and no one answered. I really wish I had been able to open up to someone about my illness, but the words would not come out because I had no idea what was happening to me.

My middle sister remembers that time: "During this time, Samantha became very introverted. Our parents did not share the details of her condition with me. I do remember that she often wore dark colours and wanted to be alone. She was not very talkative and it didn't seem like she wanted to be around people...I was concerned for her wellbeing."

But still, I refused to see a psychiatrist.

And then...onto third year. Bad choice number three. By this time, I was honestly gone. I tried to go to class but could not. I wanted my degree so badly, but completing it was not in the cards for me. My parents knew something was really wrong when my eldest sister had a baby and they could not get a hold of me by phone. My eldest sister said,

At that time, Samantha was at university in Eastern Ontario. During my pregnancy, she would barely call. We thought that she was just busy studying hard and enjoying university life. I knew something was wrong when she did not phone or call any of us on the day of my son's birth. We all tried to call her, and she was not responding. I remember sitting in the hospital, being so happy that I had a new and healthy baby boy, but feeling sad as I knew that something was wrong with my little sister Sam.

At this point my parents and I agreed that it was time for me to go home. And that is what I did. I went home and the paranoia subsided a little (I still have the paranoia to this day, but I am able to manage it) and I finally agreed to see a psychiatrist. My eldest sister said,

> My parents drove up to the university and took Samantha home. There was something wrong with her, but they didn't know what it was. This must have been extremely hard for my parents and I admire their strength and courage through all of this. We did have some history of mental illness on both sides of our family but were not sure what it all was about. Mental illness was not talked about like it is now.

> That year was a hard one for our family. I remember at my son's baptism, Samantha was there, and I could see that she was lost. I did think to myself maybe she was on drugs, as we really did not know what was going on. She wore a lot of black back then and was a heavy smoker. I remember her just sitting at a table and she would just stare and giggle.

To give you an idea of what day-to-day life with these conditions can be like, I'll let my father describe one incidence of paranoia:

> On the way back from meeting with the first Christian counsellors..., Samantha and I had an argument and she told her mom and I that the police had a warrant for her arrest. So she kept looking for police cars. We knew this was not the case, but she insisted that it was true at this time. I played handball at the YMCA with...the police chief. I had his cell number and called him to ask a favour – to check their system to see if there was a warrant for Samantha's arrest. He checked their system for her and told her that there was no warrant for her arrest. He actually spoke to her on my cell.

My brother-in-law describes a similar incident:

> We were driving around with Samantha and our daughter in the backseat. Samantha asked if I could speed up because "we are being followed." Of course, we were all startled. I looked around to see if anything looked suspicious, but it didn't. She went on to tell us that she was being followed by the

Royal Family, that they had been following her for a while. At this point, our concern skyrocketed.

The psychiatrist put me on medication. I started to improve somewhat – maybe twenty percent. I still had a long road ahead of me. At one point I tried a naturopath, but he didn't really help me. Again, I was not in this world but in another, so I wasn't able to truly recover naturally because I wasn't able to comprehend what was needed for me to get better or what I was supposed to do to recover naturally.

One thing I did learn from the naturopath, though, was to always "let it out," meaning fart! It is good for you, the naturopath told my parents. A little humour in all the hell helped me a lot, even just for a moment, to forget what I was going through. He would fart and my parents and I would laugh during the car ride home from his office, talking about the extremely loud fart we had heard. In those moments of laughter, maybe I felt a little less broken.

My lowest point was one time when my mom was making me a smoothie with all the naturopathic pills. She passed it to me, I drank it, and then I went to sit outside on our small deck and gaze at the lake. I threw up on the deck and just sat there. I did not care that I threw up. I wiped my mouth but did not move. My mom came running out and grabbed the hose. I felt nothing, because I was not truly there. That is probably when I hit rock bottom, looking at the vomit with no emotion, no feeling, just sitting there watching my mom clean it up. I was thinking of nothing, feeling nothing. It was like my soul was lost and I was just an empty body.

Around this time, I had our house blessed by a priest. I thought there were spirits around, because I could hear them and see them. It was quite real to me.

The voices I heard where very quiet and to me they sounded like spirits in another world. I was not really afraid of them, but at the same time I didn't really like them. I remember them saying something to me but I didn't quite understand. I remember hearing "go, go, go" and "no, no, no" over and over again. I don't know what the "go" and "no" meant. I did feel like I was hearing another dimension, though. Or maybe not; I'm not really sure. But at the time I heard the voices, they were so real to me.

Western medicine diagnosed me with schizophrenia. But so many other things were happening with me. I feel like I may have seen God. I definitely saw something I cannot explain; I don't really think anyone would be able to truly explain what I saw. Maybe it was a hallucination or maybe it was God. I like both theories.

What I heard and what I saw were very intriguing to me. They made me want to question things and maybe see things from different perspectives. And they made me realize that maybe sometimes two different opinions and theories can be right at the same time. My illness may have given me a better perspective on this world and let me see that different opinions and thoughts are all based on perspective.

Maybe I have schizophrenia or maybe I saw and heard God. You can take that any way you like. And I am okay with both theories being right.

Hearing voices was a very strange experience for me. I never want to experience the voices again but the experience and the voices maybe helped me see the world a little differently.

Hearing voices and having hallucinations made me a more compassionate and caring person. I pray every day that no one experiences what I experienced. I know people will experience this, but it was scary and not something a young person should ever have to go through.

This illness was the worst feeling I have ever had. I was twenty. I had my whole life ahead of me and instead I was facing something I had absolutely no idea how to face. I could see my body and I was physically there, but I was empty and lifeless, almost dead in some ways. I do not really know where my mind was or what world I was in, but I clearly was not in ours.

Chapter 3.
My Journey

I am still me.

After a long time on a waiting list, I was admitted to the Cleghorn Early Psychosis Intervention Program at St. Joseph's Hospital in Hamilton, Ontario. This is where I was diagnosed with schizophrenia. When I first heard my diagnosis, I cried. I cried because I finally knew what happened to me. And I knew from this moment I would fight to survive this illness, I would fight every single minute of every day to make it through this.

My mother explains,

> There was a program we heard about, the Cleghorn Program. My husband tried everything he could to get her in. I felt bad because I constantly asked him to check if there was an opening. We knew we had to do more. We finally got her into the Cleghorn Program and after a few appointments, it was heartbreaking when they confirmed her diagnosis as schizophrenia. As much as I had a feeling that was what it was, I wished it was not happening to her but to me instead.
>
> Samantha and I met weekly with the team and it was very hard sometimes, but a worthwhile process. The hardest part for me was when they told me I had to mourn the daughter, the person, she was. This I had trouble doing and I could not accept it. I knew in my heart I would have her back again. There was a lot of praying and asking God for help on this journey. The long process to her healing began.

My mother actually didn't tell me a lot of what was said in her meetings with the support person at the Cleghorn Program. It's sad that they told my

Embracing Schizophrenia

mom to mourn the person I was because I was such a beautiful, loving and honest child. Thinking of this now I need to tell you that I feel like I am still me, I am that kid who was kind, honest, generous, loving and good. A little bit of me will always be lost in my illness but a lot of me is a better person because of my illness.

With the help of my parents, my psychiatrist, my nurse and many others, I started to come back into this world. The medication was working, and my mind eventually started the re-entering process. I went for appointments every week at the Cleghorn Program and they gave me advice and told me what to do to recover. Everyone at the Cleghorn Program, including my psychiatrist and nurse, were amazing through all of this and they helped me so greatly and guided me on how to re-integrate into this world. Everyone at the program gave me amazing advice, but I did not really listen to them at first.

"Exercise, Samantha. You have to eat healthy too," my nurse would say. Well okay, but I can barely brush my teeth, and you expect me to take advice about exercising and eating healthy? I am lucky if I can shower in the morning.

However, my parents and doctors continually urging me to exercise and eat healthy was the right thing for them to do. "Just keep pounding it into her," I think is what they thought, "and eventually she might catch on."

Well, eventually I did, and it was a complete revelation.

If my current recovered self could tell my newly diagnosed self something, it would be to exercise and eat healthy. I wish I had listened to everyone a bit earlier. But it is never too late to figure life out! Even if you don't figure it out until you're eighty, as long as you figure it out, that's all that matters. There is no timeline for understanding life, in my opinion. I do believe, though, that it's a bonus if you can figure it out earlier.

My parents helped me immensely throughout my illness. They took me to every appointment. My mom did everything with me. She saw how broken I was, and it just about killed her, but she knew I could get through it. I am thankful every day for her support.

My mother and father were my only friends during this time. The rest of my family were busy with their lives. And to be honest, no one really understood mental illness, and of course they were a little scared of me.

I guess that is the stigma of having a mental illness. No one understands it. And I felt I had no right to tell anyone to stop living their life on my account.

Eventually I learned that everyone was praying for me and hoping I would recover, so I know now they really did care about me and love me and want the best for me, and maybe all they needed to do for me was pray that I would be okay.

My eldest sister reflects on how hard it was for the family – and the fact that people didn't talk about mental illness:

> I feel regret that I was not there for her more when she was sinking. I had two young children, a husband, and a full-time job, building up the business, me at corporate and my husband at the franchise level. I was even upset and slightly mad that my mom was not able to help me when my son was born, but she was too busy helping Samantha and being that friend to Samantha that she needed. Shame on me for feeling that way! My parents also remained positive and did not really tell us how large the issue was. They did not tell us it was schizophrenia until a few years later.

So many unknowns surround mental illness. People wonder what they should do. Should I go over?

Will she hurt me? How can I help her? I think everyone was thinking about me during this time, they just did not understand how to handle my illness. One cousin, who is like a sister to me, said she recalls meeting up with me and knowing something was going on with me but not knowing what it was.

> I knew she was suffering and something was wrong but I didn't know what was happening or what that something was. We met up from time to time and a lot of the time we would sit in silence, from what I remember. I tried to ask questions and sometimes Samantha would answer but she would take a second to answer and sometimes it wasn't answering the question I asked. I wanted to hug her and ask if she was okay but I didn't know how that would go.

But I had no idea either, and my parents had no idea. I'm pretty sure my sisters, family and friends had no idea. But with time, my family and my friends became the most supportive people in my life, and I am grateful every day for their support, especially their support of me being open about my illness. My middle sister has said that she thinks it is good that I have acknowledged what I went through and can help other people to overcome their illnesses.

I think one issue with mental illness is that there is still the unknown element, and you cannot help someone if you do not understand what they are going through or if you can't see their illness. People often fear the unknown.

My sisters are now my biggest fans. They were doing things that mattered to me when I was ill. My eldest sister was starting a family and working with my father to grow the family business, and my middle sister was working to become a lawyer.

My sisters and their partners and my nieces and nephews have brought so much joy to my life, and I thank them every day for being part of my recovery. I also have a few close friends who can talk openly about my mental illness. I am grateful every day for them.

Remember, everywhere I go and with everyone I meet, what do I talk about? You know! Talking openly with my family and friends about mental illness and mental health has honestly been the best experience of my recovery and it has made me love my family and friends so much more.

Now, whenever I speak openly, it's just Sam being Sam. They are used to me now and I am so grateful!

My mother was and is my best friend, and a funny story that she and I laugh about to this day demonstrates her dedication. In the dead of winter, I absolutely loved doing water aerobics, and my mother would come with me to the classes and participate. Years later, she told me she hated it: "Cold water and winter are two things I hate!" She froze (because Canadian winters in bathing suits are probably not the best idea, even at the pool), but she knew the classes made me feel better. So we laughed about it later. Finding humour in all of this truly has helped me.

When my mom went golfing, I would sit in the golf cart while she and her friends played. After driving the cart for my mom for so long, I decided maybe I would take up the sport and play too. Now it is one of my favourite sports. My dad says I'm a natural! I love golf and the etiquette of the sport. In golf, everyone is welcome now. Running is similar to golf in that it's inclusive and accepting and that's why I love both sports! You can walk, jog, run and do high-intensity interval training at any running race. Everyone is accepted, and that is what brought me to love running and participating in races. It is the same reason I love golf – anyone can do it. I wish everyone understood the joy of golf, because it is amazing.

My mom knew what she was doing. She thought maybe if I just went to golf with her, eventually I would start exercising, and she was right. She said,

> During these months I tried different things to try and get her more active. She was a dancer all through her youth and I think when she went away to university, she was so intent on studying that she did not take the time for physical activities. I think the stress of school and being away from home all played a part in her illness. I tried to get her to play golf, which took a whole summer of her sitting on the cart watching me, but it did pay off. The next year she began to play and now enjoys it a lot. Being out in the fresh air and just thinking about hitting that stupid little ball does wonders.

Once I started to understand the importance of exercise it became a key part of my recovery. My nurse and psychiatrist at the Cleghorn Program told me never to forget to exercise. I did not quite understand at the time, but now I get it. You will too; just keep reading.

After a few years with the Cleghorn Program (I'm not sure how long) I was introduced to someone who would help me go back to university. I was surprised that I would be able to go back so soon, but I was one hundred percent ready (well, maybe my heart was, but my mind might have needed a bit more time). Receiving a university degree was my initial goal and I was overjoyed when my doctors initiated the conversation to have me go back to school and complete my degree. It meant everything to me, even though I still was not fully here – my concentration was at about twenty or thirty percent. But I still felt that joy and that determination, which of course meant I was re-entering the world.

With a bit of help, I did return to school on a letter of permission and completed a three-year chemistry degree. (A letter of permission is a special agreement to have previously completed courses count toward a degree from another university.)

That sounds simple, right?

It turned out to be very, very complicated. It took me three years to complete the final year to earn a three-year degree. I had originally been admitted to a four-year (honours) degree program. But my original school in Eastern Ontario would not allow me to complete my four-year degree at a different university, so my dream essentially died. My parents were too afraid to have me leave home

Embracing Schizophrenia

again anyway, so I had to agree to complete courses for a three-year degree, under a letter of permission, at a university closer to home. It made me so sad.

That was twenty years ago, and things were so different then. If this had happened to me today, I think I would have been able to complete my four-year degree at a different school. And probably hell would have been raised if the school hadn't allowed me to complete the degree I was admitted for because of a mental health condition. As I said, I've had to forgive a lot of people, and that is what I did.

I forgave. I forgot. And I moved on with my life.

My experience during the three years at university closer to home on the letter of permission was tough. I failed a course. I was doing a degree on my own, no tutor, no parents to help me, with poor concentration and a serious mental illness. Navigating the university system was difficult on my own. Completing a university degree is difficult enough when you are completely healthy, never mind when you're recovering from a mental illness. If you have ever completed a degree with any illness, I commend you, because it is very difficult.

During my second year, I took one extra course because I thought I was feeling better and had done pretty well the year before. That was not the brightest idea. I knew I was going to fail that course, and I could have dropped the course to avoid receiving a failing grade, but I didn't do so by the drop date because I was navigating a world I wasn't comfortable in. I tried to appeal the failing grade, but the appeal was denied.

It's okay, though. I have moved on from a lot of things that happened in my past. I am still trying to heal, but I understand that the past is in the past and that is where it belongs.

After I failed the course, an academic advisor for the chemistry program told me that if I did not get a transcript from my previous university to him that very day, I would not be allowed to move on with my studies and I would not graduate. He wanted me to prove that my grades at my first school were good. I had to call the Eastern Ontario university and ended up with people angry at me.

That day, I talked to my cousin. I was sitting in the middle of the university campus, and I just cried. I knew this world was going to be tough, especially with a mental illness, but it was tougher than I imagined.

Move forward a year. I didn't let the academic advisor who said I wouldn't graduate deter me from my goals. It was just another roadblock I had to get past. You know what? I graduated with a three-year Bachelor of Science degree. I graduated, while still not fully recovered, and I achieved my goal.

In this life, you are going to have to let go of a lot. Holding onto pain and anger does you no good and it only lets the people who caused that anger win. Again, if this had happened to me in the present time, things would have been very different, but it was a different time, and it's pain that I no longer feel or care to waste my energy on.

Chapter 4.
Planes, Trains
and Automobiles

Rationalizing the
irrational is difficult.

So. Schizophrenia. Plus anxiety and obsessive-compulsive disorder. Enough said, right?

I wish I could say that and just end the chapter, because if you have ever experienced anxiety or obsessive-compulsive disorder (OCD), you will know that they are not pretty and they are not fun; both can be downright debilitating, pretty much just like any other mental illness. But I will discuss my daily life with anxiety and OCD and how, with time, I have learned to live with these conditions. It has not been easy, but it has become manageable.

I did not originally have anxiety with my initial diagnosis of schizophrenia. It developed over the years, and my mother and I think it had something to do with the medication I am on. I was never officially diagnosed with anxiety, but my psychiatrist has been aware of it from the beginning and recommended that I not take medication for it, which I completely agree with. She recommended that I just live with the anxiety and learn to manage it.

And then there is the OCD. I specifically suffer from driver's OCD. I don't know if that is the formal name of this form of OCD, but that's what it is known as and what I call it (it is also called hit-and-run OCD). You likely haven't heard of it — most people I tell have no idea what it is.

A lot of my anxiety is around travel. I had always liked nice long drives, but as soon as I became ill, cars became a problem for me. I would refuse to get into a car even if someone else was driving, and I would not get in the car if it was raining. It made me so anxious that it completely took over my life. My mother eventually took away my keys. I could not bear to get into a vehicle.

I become extremely nervous when flying, to the point that I am exhausted by the time the flight is done. It absolutely wipes me out.

I am pretty good on trains once I'm aboard, but I still become anxious that I will miss my stop, and getting to the train station causes anxiety, just like getting to the airport.

Though I do better with trains, my family was very nervous about me travelling by train while I was ill. My brother-in-law describes one particular trip:

> One time we all went to Florida for a vacation. Samantha was scared of flying at this point and insisted on taking the Amtrak train – on her own! I remember how relieved we all were when she made it to Florida, safe and somewhat sound...Her trip back was equally stressful for the family. I will never forget how worried I was taking her to the train station and watching her board the train, alone! I will also never forget how relieved I was when I heard she had made it home, alone!

My mother says she can't believe she and my father let me make that trip alone – my family was incredibly worried. I did miss one connection, but

I made it in the end. My father says that was a scary time, though.

On the trip home from Florida, the train was delayed and I missed the connecting train at New York's Grand Central Station. I was in the busiest station I had ever been in! I found an office, where there was an older man. I told him I had missed my train and asked if he could help me with a hotel. He was the kindest, sweetest person I had encountered. I know he knew I was ill but he didn't say anything about it. He just took me to the hotel, paid for the room and told me, "You better be on that train in the morning." I said I would be.

This encounter reminded me about kindness, that you never truly know what someone is feeling or going through in life. The man's kindness made me feel somewhat normal, and I hate using the world normal, but he just helped me. I wish I could find him or his family and let them know how much he helped me that day. I did email Amtrak; I hope they received the message.

Also on the train from Florida to New York, I got my period, and of course because I was ill, I had no idea when my period was coming. I had to use toilet paper! After I was in the hotel and had dinner, I had to go to a pharmacy and get pads. I just walked out of the hotel in the middle of New York and bought pads and went right back to the hotel. I went to sleep and caught the train to Buffalo early in the morning.

The trip wasn't all bad: I played cards on the train with two people I met and it was so much fun!

The night before any travel, I do not sleep at all. My mind races through all the scenarios, then my heart pounds and I start to breath heavily, and I know it is my anxiety. Then I am wide awake at midnight, thinking to myself, why can I not just sleep? That is all I want to do, but the anxiety pretty much takes control and I lie there until morning. So I get on my phone (and thank goodness for phones; honestly, I know social media isn't great sometimes, but for someone who doesn't sleep, the phone sometimes is a blessing and a distraction).

If I have to fly, the nervousness sets in right when I'm getting ready to go to the airport. My mind thinks of every scenario: we are going to miss the flight if the airport is busy, so maybe we should get picked up just a half-hour earlier. So then we get picked up and get to the airport three hours before the flight! I always say to my parents, "Well, better we wait there than at home," but thinking to myself, clearly I am not going to miss this flight.

And then comes the flight itself. I try to distract myself most of the time by going on my computer or watching TV. It does work and I keep to myself, and manage to be happy by the time we land.

Then after travelling by train or plane, by about 8 p.m. that night, the exhaustion sets in and I fall asleep. My body basically shuts down and I sleep, and once morning comes the next day, I am back to being content – and happy I am not travelling.

I have met so many amazing people on my mental health journey, like the kind man at the train station. Another was a flight attendant on a flight to Florida. When I board a plane, I explain that I have anxiety but that I am usually pretty calm and quiet and keep to myself. Most people don't expect that, they expect me to scream and yell and wave my arms and exclaim that I want out of the plane. But this flight attendant promptly said, "I know exactly what you're talking about. My boyfriend has an illness and he does the same thing. It's all inside." And I looked at her and found some peace. I said, "Yes! That's me. I can't explain how I am feeling, it's just how I am feeling." She was so kind and reminded me that there are people in this world who are kind and really do understand mental illness. As I've been writing this book, it's been nice thinking of the people I've met along my journey.

For a very long time I did not fly because it caused me too much anxiety. With time, however, I started to learn a lot about my anxiety and how I can live with it and still manage to get to different places. I took a group anxiety class when I was at the university closer to home, and it helped me greatly. Mostly just opening up to others helped, and understanding that I am not in this alone. It was nice to know that people struggled just like me and that they could overcome so much, just like me.

After participating in that group, and with a lot of reflection, I eventually decided that I would fly again. My first trip was to New York City. I was terrified, but I got on the plane and got to the hotel in one piece. Calmness came over me when I reached the hotel. My mom and dad, two sisters, and their families came with me to support me. It was my first flight in, I think, five years and I think they were really proud of me.

My mom describes one great trip we did when I was feeling better: "We had ten days in Europe and took six planes. We visited London first, which was filled with fun. Then off to Germany to visit my mother's birthplace, which was so wonderful to see. Our last stop was Italy to visit with my husband's relatives. So much good food and fun again."

I have learned that if I want to get to different places, if I want to see the world or have a vacation, the only way I can do that is to take a train, plane or automobile. I cringe every time I think about travel. I love it so much, but it also gives me so much anxiety!

Sometimes with driving my mind wins and I choose not to go anywhere, but I have yet to miss a plane or a train because of my anxiety. I am pretty proud of myself for this, because I have not let the anxiety win.

I guess what travelling has taught me is to tell myself that I know I am going to get anxious, but I can handle my anxiety and I know that once the travel is over and I go to sleep, I will be fine. Yes, I may have an anxious day but I will get through it. I will exercise in the morning and hopefully my anxiety will subside. I basically talk to myself and tell myself that this anxiety is not going to stop me from living my life, even if I do not sleep or if I am exhausted. My anxiety will never win.

About three or four years ago, I started thinking I had gone through a red light, and I thought maybe I had hit someone. I would go back and check to see if anyone had been hit or if there were ambulances at the spot I thought the accident had happened. I did not quite know what was happening to me, so I turned to our favourite search engine and I googled what I was feeling. And lo and behold, what I was feeling was driver's obsessive-compulsive disorder! I love that we can do research so easily nowadays.

I brought up the problem with my counsellor and she has discussed my driver's OCD with me. Number one, she said, "Samantha, are you the type of person who would go through a red light?" I said no, of course not, I would never go through a red light. And she replied, "Think about that. Clearly you are not going through red lights." (She was right.) And number two, she told me to stop going back and checking to see if I had hit a person or a car. Not checking was the most difficult part for me (but again, she was right).

So with time, I forced myself to not check. I still sometimes call my parents and tell them I'm scared and I ramble on that I might have hit someone, and they try to calm me down by telling me, "Sam, you would know if you hit someone," and then with time and with a little talking to myself, I realize I did not hit anyone or anything and that I did the right thing by not going back and checking.

It is difficult sometimes because I like driving but at the same time I do not like driving. Through counselling, I have learned not to check anymore. I have trained myself to hear my counsellor's voice: "Samantha, you did not hit anything or anyone, do not check, drive to where you are going." And that is what I do. I do become stressed, thinking I hit something or someone, but those feelings eventually dissipate, and I work through my feelings around the OCD and I return to some sense of being okay again.

Anxiety and OCD can be overwhelming at times. I do believe, however, that with work and talking through the anxiety and the OCD, even to yourself, you can manage it. Rationalizing the irrational is difficult, but I do know it can be done because I have done it. Don't get me wrong, things are far from perfect. I have days when I wish I could just stay in bed and not deal with this world or my illnesses, but I know the best thing for me is to go out and live with it.

I listened to my psychiatrist, I learned to live with it and manage it, and that is what I do to the best of my ability. So far, it has worked for me. All I need is a chauffeur and maybe my life would be a little easier!

Chapter 5.
I'd Like My Four-Year Degree, Please

There may be obstacles, and it may take me longer, but I will never give up.

After I graduated with a three-year Bachelor of Science degree, I worked for my father in his auto-industry business. It was a great experience. I always tell people that to recover, you need to, number one, exercise; number two, eat healthy; and number three, work and socialize (number four is spirituality, but we will get to that). Working let me socialize, and that helped me recover.

Something in my life was missing, however; something was not complete. I realized it was the fact that I had originally been accepted to a four-year (honours) degree program but was not allowed to complete a four-year degree on the letter of permission at the university closer to my home.

So after working with my father for about three years, I applied to more universities. I was accepted to a few and chose to do my four-year science degree with a major in applied mathematics at a University in Toronto.

My parents were so afraid for me moving away – my mom says they wondered if the pressure would be too much, even though they felt I was ready to be on my own. My father says they believed in me and trusted me despite their concern. I don't think they realized how much this independence would help my recovery. Being on my own allowed me to learn, surprisingly, what recovery really was and why we do not one hundred percent focus on recovery in this world. We talk a lot about illnesses and the way we are feeling, but we do not talk a lot about having a truly successful recovery.

Although the doctors said I was recovered when I returned to university to complete my first degree, I don't think I was fully recovered. I sometimes still don't think I am entirely recovered, probably because recovery is not perfect at all times and is not linear. But is anything?

The recovery I am in allows me to live in this world with a mental illness. There are bad days and hard days, but there are good days too.

I had a great experience at university when I did my four-year math degree. The administration understood that I had a mental illness and I needed assistance, especially with studying and exams. I would walk to school every day through downtown Toronto. This is when I grew to love the city. Everything was around me.

I used my savings to pay for rent and tuition. My parents helped me with rent during my last year because I had no money left. However, having a small amount of money to work with meant I learned to budget while I lived in Toronto. Then I learned about running and also about healthy food. And this was the breakthrough point for me. I was either going to successfully recover or I was going to stumble and fall. This was the point where my life changed again, except instead of losing everything, I gained everything.

Toronto was where I mastered running. My mom would always say, "Sam, just go for a run.

Trust me, you will feel better." She was one hundred percent right. If I can tell you anything, listen to your mom! Listen to the people and professionals around you because they know what they are talking about.

At this university I met by best friend. She is the most amazing friend in the world. I have never met a friend I trusted this completely, and I am forever grateful for her support and friendship.

I spent time with another friend during my time in Toronto. Although we are no longer close, I have always thought she was an amazing person and I deeply care for her to this day. I have always wanted the best for her. Sometimes relationships and friendships take different paths. I am hoping ours eventually cross again but if not, I will understand that the universe has a plan for us.

After four years of studying, running, eating healthy and focusing on recovery, in the spring of 2013, I graduated with an honours Bachelor of Science degree in applied mathematics.

I decided to do another Bachelor's degree in science for many reasons. The first was to show the university I attended in Eastern Ontario, which would not allow me to do a four-year degree, that my new degree trumps the three-year degree they "allowed" me to do. The second reason was that I truly love science, especially mathematics. I believe that if you love something, you should follow what you love, and science was in my heart. During my first degree, before I became ill, I was actually going to change my major from chemistry to a dual chemistry and mathematics major. I never did get that chance, so that is why I chose to do a mathematics major for my second degree.

Working toward this degree was so different from my first degree. My professors knew that near the end of my studies I was struggling and they showed me more compassion. They knew I was a good student and that I was going through something and knew that sometimes all someone needs is a little compassion. With their help I completed my last semester and graduated.

It's hard to explain how much this meant to me. I was still managing my illness, so not everything was perfect (is it ever?) but I accomplished what I set out to do. I finally felt complete. And I now knew I could do a Master's degree if I wanted to.

I did try a Master's program, but it was not right for me at that time. I moved closer to home after graduation to complete the Master's program. I had struggled a bit in my last semester at the school in Toronto, and four months into the Master's program I had to leave.

This was the time when I was between school and work. I called my psychiatrist and asked her if she could help me get onto disability assistance. Instead, she gave me the best advice ever. She said, "You can work, Samantha," and she was right. So I decided to work for my father again. It was good for me and I continue to this day to work with my dad. I am still planning on doing my Master's degree, most likely in business.

I plan to complete that degree a little later in life. Time is irrelevant to me now. If I want to do something, I am going to do it, whether I am twenty or forty or eighty. Let no one tell you you can't do something because of your age. You can do whatever you want at any age and at any time in your life.

You can do anything you set your mind to. I completed my first degree with a serious mental illness and I completed my second degree with a serious mental illness, lightly recovered and all on my own. I will never, ever let anyone tell me I can't do something. There may be obstacles, and it may take me a lot longer than everyone else, but I will do what I put my mind to and I believe everyone can.

Chapter 6.
#Running and #Walking – Love Your Body!

Run a marathon, they said. It will be fun, they said!

My doctors said the same thing my mom told me: you need to exercise. You need to move, you need to work out. It will help you and your mind. I did not truly comprehend what everyone was saying to me. Then in Toronto I started to walk and run. If I could tell my younger self, my deeply struggling mentally ill self, anything at all, I would say you should work out. It will help your recovery so much more than you know.

I wish I had understood the link between mental health and exercise when I was really ill because it would have made an enormous difference in my life and in my recovery. It would have made my life easier. I honestly believe running and walking brought me back to this world.

Have you ever heard of runner's high? It is amazing. And it works, especially if you have a mental illness.

You do not need to run a marathon or even five kilometres to get runner's high. All you need to do is a short, fast run and you will experience it. It is the most incredible feeling. It gives you a sense of inner peace and inner calmness. It usually happens after any high-intensity workout. I tell everyone about it, because to get through life we all need a little bit of runner's high.

Once I had a taste of running, it became a large part of my life and my recovery. I started running short distances, which I still love to do, and once I moved to Toronto, I really became a runner. Having a gym in my condominium building made it easier for me to walk and run on the treadmill. And then I began to see a whole community of people who loved to walk, run and work out. It was like my eyes were suddenly open to the amazingness of the fitness world.

In Toronto, I would walk to school every day. On weekends I would usually run in the mornings and I felt invigorated, like I could take on the world. I loved it. If you've had this feeling after exercise, you will understand what I am saying.

After a run, I felt that life was just a little easier, or at least my day was going to be a little easier. It was almost like the run was a pill: run for fifteen minutes and your mind will feel the difference. I could not believe how much walking and running helped my mind. It was an incredible awakening for me to the world of exercise and the connection it has to the mind.

I forget exactly how I started to participate in running races, but I think my first race was either the 5K Around the Bay race in Hamilton with my eldest sister or the 5K Scotiabank Waterfront race in Toronto with my cousin. What matters is the effect these races had on me. Both changed my life.

Once I discovered running races, I loved them. There was something about race day that I connected to. I have always loved that anyone can run or walk. Running and racing are inclusive, accepting and completely positive. All you have to do is buy a pair of running shoes or find a pair at a thrift store (that is why I always donate my running shoes). Even if you do not race, you can still walk or run on your own time. I think that is the greatest part of the sport.

The best part of race day is the positivity. That's what made me fall in love with race day — the way so many people can come together and have this amazing energy around them is invigorating and it fuelled my passion for running. Even in the worst weather and maybe even the worst times of our lives, running allows everyone to have this beautiful sense of positivity, even for just one day or one run.

I started with five kilometre races. I figured if I could do five kilometres I am all set. However, all those five kilometre races turned into me thinking maybe I wanted to do a ten kilometre, which turned into me thinking, well, I haven't done a half marathon yet, that's the next race up from a ten kilometre, so maybe I should do that. And so it went. My wonderful running journey was underway.

I participated in two half marathons. And after running those, my sister said we had done so many five kilometre races that maybe it was time for something else. She said, "Sam, why don't we do an Iron Girl race together?"

I agreed and it was the most amazing experience. I swam in Lake Ontario, biked twenty kilometres and then ran five kilometres. After the race, I felt like I could do and accomplish anything. I had never felt this before even in all my running races. The Iron Girl reminded me that anything is possible.

After the Iron Girl, I thought well, it is finally the right time for me to do a marathon. So I ran my first marathon and it was incredible. Yes, it was difficult. It poured rain at the start and continued raining for almost the whole time. At many points I struggled. I felt sick during the last hour, yet I never thought to myself that I would not finish. I crossed that finish line, wet, cold and with a sore stomach, but I am proud to say I ran my first marathon! The marathon reminded me that no matter what we face – rain, wind, illness – we have a desire to survive and succeed. I cannot really explain why I kept going, I just did.

My goal in all my races is just to train. Sure, I love race day and the positivity around it and crossing the finish line, but I always tell people, if there is no race day, at least you got up, you put on your running shoes and you tried. You do not have to finish the race and you do not have to run a marathon. All that matters is that you ran, and you tried.

Running with a mental illness is difficult at times, but I love that I listen to the voice in my head that tells me every morning to get up and train, that even if I'm exhausted, I should still put on my running shoes and run. There is always another voice in the morning while I am in bed saying, "Just stay here, just stay in bed, relax, have breakfast, watch the news." And sometimes that voice wins, but that's usually my body telling me to rest. Most days, though, I do not listen to that voice, I listen to the one that tells me I will feel so much better after a run. So I run.

It seems like I have taught my mind or my body that running and exercise will help my mental health. Eventually running and working out became a coping mechanism for me. I came to know that exercising would help my mind, and my body recognizes when I need to run. Running is probably the number one reason my recovery has been successful. There have been days when I have been so unhappy, I have felt stress and high anxiety, and somehow my mind knows that running will help, so I put on my running shoes and go for a run. After fifteen minutes of running, those feelings have eased a little.

My mind and my body know I have to run when I am struggling, because I know I will feel better and have a better day because of that run. My father says I've trained my mind like someone who plays piano. Eventually your body takes over and you just know how to play the piano. That is what happens to me with running: my body knows I will feel better after running, so it makes me run. Eventually it just became part of my daily life. Running is one of the key ways I have learned to manage my mental illness.

My life changed the minute I discovered how to make my mental health better through exercise. I truly believe you can train yourself to cope with mental illness and with life in general.

People around me noticed the difference exercise made. My niece said, "She has also taken matters into her own hands by focusing on her health – body, mind and soul...Her dedication and passion for running and promoting movement as a tool in her recovery journey I know has had an impact on those around her who are also struggling."

My mom knew that while I was in Toronto I did a lot of walking. She agrees this is where my love of running really started. She sees that walking and running have been great help to my recovery.

Recovery will not happen in a day or a week. It may take years. I believe, however, that we can learn ways to manage.

One of the best ways to start running or working out is to set a goal to motivate yourself. I do like signing up for races because it gives me a distance goal and it motivates me to wake up in the mornings and run – maybe even a little longer than before. But you do not have to sign up for a race. Just pick a date and set a goal that by that date you will be at a particular time or distance or pace. Goals for working out truly help motivate you in the worst of times. I wish someone had told me that years ago, because the first thing I would have done was sign up for a five kilometre run.

My doctors always talked to me about exercise, but they also always, always spoke to me about food. And again, I did not really pay attention to them at first. I have found, however, that focusing on food and how it affects the mind has been another big part of my recovery. Food and the mind are a very difficult subject to discuss, like exercise and fitness. There are many different theories. Let me explain my thoughts on food and how I have come to manage my mental health with food.

What we eat does affect our mind and our mood. I truly believe this. I am not saying eat salad all the time, I am saying feed yourself good food most of the time and your mind may actually benefit.

I feel like there is a disconnect between the mind and food in our society and in the world. It's like we know that if we eat healthy food we will feel better, but we choose not to eat well. I don't really know why, because we all know the connection is there. We need to end this disconnect. Understand that your mental health recovery can be affected by food.

It's unrealistic in this world to eat healthy all the time; however, you need to know that healthy foods are actually beneficial for your mind. Just don't exert too much control over your food, meaning if you want to eat a piece of pie or a few pieces of pizza, you should have a piece of pie or some pizza. There needs to be a happy and healthy balance with food. I believe trying too intensely to control food will lead to disordered eating.

I had struggled with food since I was a teenager, and my mother points out that I had gained weight because of my medications. I have been on a food journey since 2011. I lost a significant amount of weight in 2011 and was really focused on healthy eating – maybe a little too focused. But of course, with life comes lessons, and if you do not learn from your lessons, there is no ability to grow and be better. So, one good lesson was loving my body.

My counsellor introduced me to a new way of looking at and thinking about my body and with time, it completely changed my outlook on health and food, and it made me realize how obsessed our world is with diet culture and how negative that obsession is.

I have learned on my food journey that I have to do what is right for me, not what is right for anyone else. I still calorie count, but I focus on nourishing and fuelling my body.

My goal is healthy eating, nourishing my body and doing what feels right for my body.

I now look at food as something to nourish and fuel. I don't eat a lot of sugar anymore. I eat mostly healthy foods. I have been a vegetarian since I was seventeen and I also now do not eat a lot of dairy foods. I became a vegetarian because I did not want animals to be killed. Now that I'm older and have researched health and fitness, I have learned that a vegetarian diet is actually quite healthy. So now I am a vegetarian because I want to save animals and because I want to be healthy.

When I lost the weight and embraced my body as it is, I realized I still had a disordered way of looking at food. With some reflection, I now try to eat only foods that nourish my body, and thus, I also eat foods to nourish my mind. My niece told me she notices that I have chosen to fuel my body with foods that nourish and support internal healing. For me, this is the best way to look at food. Before, I looked at food as either calories or as something of which I could eat as much as I wanted and not think about my body or mind.

I do not agree with dieting and diet culture. I know many people – friends, family and acquaintances – who are constantly on restrictive diets. I do not even really know why they are. We are so obsessed with what our bodies should look like that we forget what we are doing to our bodies with dieting.

I do not believe in diets at all. I feel like they have a negative influence on how we view our bodies. I know people who have been on a diet their whole life and to me, that's not right or fair to them. Society needs to stop advertising diets and pushing diet culture. So many people look at food in a disordered way.

At some point I started to see food in an ordered way as fuel for my body and mind and this was so freeing. I freed myself from disordered eating. Free yourself from dieting. Free yourself from the disconnect between the mind and food. I do believe that if we can free ourselves from the constraints of society and focus on healthy eating and nourishing ourselves, we can finally move away from diet culture.

I just want you to remember that looking at food as nourishment for your mind and body, in my opinion, is a great way of living a balanced life-style. It is working for me and I do believe it can work for everyone. Stop dieting. Love your body. Nourish your mind.

Chapter 7.
I'm on Medication.
Am I Mad?

Relapsing is my biggest fear.

I am on medication and I have been for a very long time. And in my opinion there is nothing wrong with that. Of course I would prefer not to have to take medication. I would very much prefer that I had never taken medication in the first place, but again, I was not in this world, so when someone told me, "Take this," I took it. I didn't know what it was, I just took it. End of story.

I don't blame anyone for putting me on medication, but if I could go back, I would do things very differently, especially in regard to medication and therapy. However, the past is in the past and that is where it belongs. My parents did tell me they tried many different treatments, including more natural methods, and nothing worked, so eventually they agreed to have me take medication.

I cannot go back and tell my younger self how to properly handle a mental illness. There are so many things I would have done differently. But I cannot make my past any different. What I know is that the medication I was given did help me at the time and in the state of mind I was in.

People sometimes ask me what to do if they are feeling mentally ill, and I always recommend that they try counselling first, before medication. I tell everyone I give advice to that it is not going to be as easy as just taking medication. Recovery is difficult and it will take time – and sometimes years to figure it out. If I could go back, I would try to put in more work when I was in the worst of my illness, because there were many things I needed to work on in my life. I did start counselling after my recovery and found it helped greatly.

I tell people to see a counsellor because I believe mental illness can sometimes stem from certain experiences we never acknowledged in our lives and counselling can help deal with those experiences. You may need to be on medication too; however, I believe that working on yourself and really understanding why you may be going through something is always the right choice before anything else. The issues are much, much deeper than we think.

It is sometimes difficult in the health and wellness world to discuss my opinion on medication, although I think really it is more about my experience with having a serious mental illness than it is about medication.

I would love to not take medication, but I have to. There is no way around it. People say to me all the time, "Maybe you should go off your medication and take a healthier approach." I love how they say "healthier" because they clearly do not get it. Here is how I handle the "you shouldn't take medication" discussion:

1. Have you ever had a mental illness? Because when I was suffering before recovery, it was absolute hell; trust me, you would not want to be there. I did not even have the mental capacity to wash my face or brush my teeth. You cannot truly know how bad it was for me

because you did not see me during those times. If I go off of this medication there is a chance that I could go back to that, and that is a risk I am not willing to take.

2. Have you ever had a bad day with a mental illness or have you been around someone who was having a bad day with a mental illness? Because trust me, it is not easy. I may have had a week when I was feeling great, and thought to myself, maybe I do not need this medication, I think I will be fine without it! Some days, I feel like I'm ready to stop taking the medication, but then I have a really rough day that reminds me of why I am taking it. I could get through the easier days without medication, but those rough days are bad and that is why I am on medication.

I do recommend to other people to try alternative medicines and natural health approaches when you are first diagnosed, but in the end you may need medication.

These are my thoughts only, and I am sure everyone else has their own thoughts on the subject. But I do recommend trying alternatives at first and then if those don't work, maybe you might need medication.

And no one ever has a right to tell anyone to stop taking medication.

I probably would not have survived the worst parts of my illness if I was not put on medication. Even if you experienced the exact same thing as I did and are not on medication, remember that every human is unique, so treatment that worked for someone else might not work for me, just as my treatment might not work even for someone else who has experienced the same symptoms. Some medications work for some people, and some do not.

There is such a stigma about medication for the mind, but I understand why I was put on medication and that is why I continue to take it.

When I was at my second university, in Toronto, I took a course about mental illness; it was amazing. It was about the history of madness and the madness movement. The madness movement does not believe in medication, which I understand. There are so many opinions for what you can do with a mental illness. What I believe is that we have to figure out our illnesses for ourselves. Yes, we will have doctors and nurses and psychiatrists, we will have family and friends, and support is very important, but to figure out what works for you, you have to listen to and trust yourself and know what is best for you. That's what I have learned.

Embracing Schizophrenia

I was given great advice and I listened to so many different opinions, but in the end, I realized that I am unique, and my recovery will also be unique to me. Sometimes we think, "Well, that medication worked for her so it should work for me," but everyone is different. When it comes to medication, it's a personal choice and it may be the only option to assist with serious illnesses.

Trust yourself. You know what is best for you. No one else does. Get in tune with your body and your soul and your mind. Listen to your support system, but remember, if someone tells you that you should go off your meds to be healthier, ask them if they have ever gone through what you are going through. All I know is that I never again want to experience what I went through, or relapse, so if that means I have to be on medication for the rest of my life, so be it.

Chapter 8.
Did God Forget
About Me?

I will always believe.
I can't wait to meet you.

This thought that creeps into people's minds sometimes – that God has abandoned them – has never
crossed my mind. Not even once. I know at times
in our lives, if we are spiritual and have faith, we
may wonder if God has forgotten us in trying
times. Trust me, God has not left us and never will.
God is always there, even at the worst of times.

I am a very spiritual person. I truly believe in a higher power, something bigger than you and me, something that makes me feel peace at certain moments of my day and my life. Before I became seriously ill, I had a strong relationship with God. I spoke to God all the time and I told God I loved Them all the time. I will always love God first and foremost before anyone or anything else in this world.

When I became ill, since I was not in this world but in another, I did not think about or talk to God like I did before I became ill. You may think God abandoned me. However, I did hallucinate, and I told my parents God was knocking on my door one night and that I saw God in the window when I was at my friend's cottage.

I didn't speak to God like I had before, but God was definitely present and around me. I did not really feel God the way I felt Them before and after my illness, but I actually saw God, which might be even better, right? It was almost as if during the worst of my illness God was somehow there with me and I did not really realize it until after my recovery. When I started to recover, I stopped seeing God (or in medical terms, hallucinating) and I again spoke to God and felt God around me like I had before my illness.

Did God Forget About Me?

It was as if during my illness God's presence somehow became stronger than it had been when I was well. I will never forget what I saw in those moments – I remember them clearly. I was lying in bed in the middle of the night, and I opened my eyes and saw a light around my door, and I heard knocking. I was so afraid someone was there that I closed my eyes and went back to bed. Sitting on the couch at the cottage, I was staring out the window when I saw this beautiful light moving around in the air. It was peaceful and bright, and it enveloped me. I turned away, not quite sure what I was seeing, and I forgot about this light for a time.

I know that God will never forget about us, that God will never forget about me, even if we think God has abandoned us. I truly believe God is always there. I did not feel God in the worst of times, but I saw God, more clearly than I have ever seen Them. God is always there. We might just have to look a bit harder for signs of God's presence. It didn't occur to me until years later that God had never left me and never will, even in my darkest times.

Although I speak about God, I should clarify that this is just the term I use. I do not believe in one God or one religion, I believe in all Gods and all religions. I believe in the power of the universe.

I believe God is part of the energy of the universe. I do not believe God is female or male; that's why I say "Them." I do not judge other religions or other people or their beliefs. I honestly believe everyone is correct in their beliefs and no one's spiritual beliefs are wrong in the eyes of the universe, as long as they are respectful, good and kind.

Some things in faith or religion or spirituality or whatever you would like to call it, I agree with and some I do not, but I do not really like to talk about what I agree with and what I don't because again, I do not judge people's beliefs and I am not "God" in this world and I have no right to tell anyone what is right or what is wrong or what to believe. Only God can make that choice.

Spirituality is a large part of my growth and throughout my years on this earth, I have seen the amazement and beauty that spirituality brings. Understanding that there is something more to this world brings a lot of peace to me and to my life. Understanding that your illness is part of a bigger plan can bring a sense of calmness, a sense of love and joy, a sense of happiness – at least, that is what it has done for me. I speak to God every day, like I did before I became ill, and I understand that God is in my heart and God is in all my choices and in every part of my being.

If I can tell you anything in your mental health recovery journey, it is to connect to a higher power. It will bring you joy and peace and give you a sense of calmness in a crazy world. But I also believe that if you never connect to a higher power that is okay too. In the end everyone makes their own choices in life and that is what is great about this world.

Just remember, though, if you do believe in God, that God is always present everywhere and at all times in our lives, even when you think God is not here.

Chapter 9.
Losing Everything

Maybe you need to lose everything to gain everything.

I lost my entire self in one moment. I truly do understand this feeling, but it is sometimes unexplainable.

Losing everything is probably one of the most terrifying life experiences, because you are truly left with nothing. You are stripped of your entire being and left with an emptiness you are not sure you can fix. You are and have nothing. When I became nothing, it was terrifying, and yet there was an odd sense of discovery in being nothing and rebuilding. It is a complicated experience.

I lost myself when I was twenty in my university dorm room. In that moment I knew I would never be the same person again, that a piece of me would always be broken, that I would never truly be myself again, because a part of me was gone.

It was terrifying and it broke me.

I did not know if I would be able to find myself again and I did not know if I would ever be unbroken. I knew it was going to take me a long time to figure out how to become me again. Rebuilding yourself is not an easy task but I now believe it can be done and that you can fix the brokenness. It took me years to figure it out, and I am still learning every day how to build myself and become better. But I need you to know you can rebuild yourself; it can be done. I know this because I did it. You can find yourself in all the madness and fear. You, your being, yourself, you are all still in there, even though it seems like you are gone or lost or broken. You are there.

In all of this, I listened to myself. I trusted myself and I rebuilt myself from nothing. And now I see the world so differently. This new view of the world I have is so amazing that I wish everyone could feel it and understand it. I live each and every day knowing that tomorrow could be my last day on earth or my last day knowing myself. I live in the present, I cherish the beauty I see in this world and I love everything about life and about what it has to offer me.

Losing myself taught me that life can be short and that if you live in the present, you truly understand life and what it means to be here. I know that anything can happen tomorrow. I could get hit by a car and die, I could become ill and not survive – anything could happen.

So you need to live for today and cherish everything in the present moment, because these moments are all that matter in life. I do believe you need to plan a little for the future, but you also need to know that you could die tomorrow. Life is always unknown and your place on earth is unknown. See the beauty in the world and in every day you have on earth, because you may not be here tomorrow.

Yes, I lost myself and I was broken, but I was given something bigger than me: I was given a viewpoint on life that not many people have, and I believe this happened to me so that I could share this viewpoint with the world. Most of us do not live our lives as if we won't be here tomorrow. There is so much planning and working and making money that we forget tomorrow may never come.

I would give anything to go back and change the day I lost everything, but I do understand why I lost everything and why this happened to me. I admit that I wish I had not gone through what I went through, because it broke me and I will probably never get back a piece of me that was lost in that moment. A piece of me is still broken, and that broken piece reminds me to live every day like it is my last and always try to be better at life.

A part of me always remembers that moment, maybe because someone – the universe, God – wants me to know that everything can change in one day. And it reminds me that losing everything taught me so much about myself, my life and how I want to live.

I do believe I lost everything so that I could gain everything.

Chapter 10.
I'm Talking about It
and I Don't Care
What You Think

I have seen beauty in
the most broken souls.
Including mine.

I have been open about my illness from the beginning, or at least from the point when I was eighty
percent back in this world and able to form my
feelings into words.

My close friend describes when I started talking about my condition to her:

I worked with a man...who would sometimes talk about things I didn't understand or just not turn up to work. I asked my boss about it and she told me...he had paranoid schizophrenia. I confessed my concerns about my friend. I described what I was noticing about Samantha and she agreed with my suspicions. She gave me some helpful advice. My concern, however, was that Samantha had not confided in me yet. I understood why. This is going back twenty years ago and people just didn't talk about it. Samantha and I were friends for so long, but that just meant that there was more at stake if Samantha confided in me and I turned my back on her. I wanted her to know that I cared and understood and would be there. So I tricked her.

I started talking about work. I told her about my co-worker. I talked about how cool it was that he was open with his illness. I talked and I talked and then Samantha talked. From then on, we were able to have open conversations about her illness and we could laugh together.

I love being open about my illness. Sometimes, when people make negative comments (I do not hear those a lot, but sometimes), it makes me want to be even more open, to throw my openness in their faces!

My all-time favourite question about my openness from people is, "Don't you care what people will think of you?"

My response?

No, I do not. People around you – friends, family and even complete strangers – will judge you no matter what you do, so you might as well do what you want and say what you want (as long as it's respectful).

Between school and work, and work and school, I decided to join a group that talks openly in different situations about their experience with mental illness. This is where I learned that being open about my illness was the best option for me and one of the most positive experiences I've had. I have never looked back. I truly believe one of the reasons my recovery has been so successful is that I have been open about my illness and I have not worried about what people think of me or the fact that I'm so open. Other people are more concerned about me being open about my mental illness than I am. Speaking openly is an amazing and beautiful experience. It showed me something I did not think I would find in my illness.

My friends and family agree about the importance of speaking out. My cousin said,

> What mental health needs is more people like Samantha, who bring the conversation to life. Showing us that without struggle there is no progress... She has been an inspiration to us all. She wants people to know it gets better, one day at a time. She wants to help those who may feel like they are silently struggling. If she can get through it, so can you. She is proving that you can live well, and overcome your fears.

I have spoken to schools, colleges, universities, families – so many people, young and old, people who have had mental illnesses or who have been touched by mental illness. One time, no one showed up to hear me speak at the school in Toronto. At first I was anxious and fearful of speaking again, but I said to myself, if you reach just one person by putting yourself in an uncomfortable situation sometimes, then that is what matters, not your pride or your ego.

What I have found through all this speaking is kindness. Speaking openly has showed me absolute human kindness, love and compassion. Many times when I have spoken, no one has said a word while I was sharing my story. Everyone listened to every sentence I said. They listened deeply and showed me the true wonder of being open and speaking the truth. It was as if people wanted to talk about mental illness, like they were intrigued by it, but they did not know where to start or what to say.

What I saw in all this was complete human compassion and kindness toward me, and I felt an energy around me, this energy I know we, as humans, are capable of.

I have seen so much beauty in the people I have talked to. I always say we are capable of so much as humans and as a community because I have seen it first hand in my experience of being open about my illness.

I have seen beauty in the most broken souls, people who think they are lost. I have looked at them and seen absolute beauty. I have seen what they are capable of, and I want them to see what I see. I believe we are capable of more love and compassion than we realize. We are capable of great success and happiness, and we also do not see that in ourselves. Let me tell you I have seen it and I have felt it in my journey of being open, and I see it in everyone who is suffering and broken.

I have chosen to be open about my experience for many reasons.

The main reason is that I do not want a single person in this world to go through what I went through. I went through hell. I felt I had lost everything in a single day and I didn't know if I would ever get it back. I lost myself – every piece of me was gone, and I had to rebuild myself, my mind and my soul, from nothing. Trust me, it was not easy. I was so lost that I cannot explain the feeling because it felt like nothingness. I do not want anyone to feel that emptiness. My goal until the day I die is to make it so that no one experiences what I experienced, that people actually get help prior to losing control. If people are informed about mental illness at an early age I truly believe this can help and that it can change the course of someone's experience with mental illness.

Another reason I am so open about my experience is hope. It seems in the world of mental health that there is a feeling of hopelessness. I felt it every single day I was suffering, and in the present day I still feel it in everything I hear and see in relation to mental illness. I just want people to have hope and to know they are going to get through this, that in this moment it may be difficult and scary and it may feel like there is no way out, but I know, from experience, it will get better, maybe even better than your life was before your illness.

I'm encouraged to know from my family and friends that my message of hope is getting through! My aunt (my father's sister) said, "You are an inspiration to your family and to many others out there who suffer from mental illness. You are a beacon of hope and light to families whose loved ones have been diagnosed with schizophrenia." My best friend agrees this is valuable: "Your openness has always given me hope, especially considering how prevalent the stigma around mental illness still is. Although you have lived through this stigma and experienced it many times in your life, you remain open and hopeful. Your journey of healing gave me and many others hope."

I am also open about mental illness because I want people to know they can recover. I guess this ties into hope. I want people to know they can manage their illness and thrive, just like me.

Those around me have come to understand the importance of me speaking out. For example, my cousin, who is as close to me as a sister, has said, "I think the more people talk about mental illness, the better people who do not suffer from it will understand it. I think people who have mental illness need voices and people who are brave, like Samantha, to advocate for them." My aunt said, "Thank you, Samantha, for breaking the silence on mental illness and for paving the road for others." Another aunt said,

> When the family finally got answers Sam started to speak about her mental illness and I attended one of her talks. It helped me understand the process and how long she and her family had been suffering. I was so proud of her because she was strong enough to share all her experiences with other young people.
>
> She continues to share all of this with a blog and I marvel at the honesty, intelligence and kind way in which she goes about it. I believe that she has helped many people see and understand the illness of schizophrenia. She is an amazing young woman.

My father said,

> Another big achievement was Samantha starting to speak publicly about her mental illness, her story and how it started, her recovery, and how she dealt with her mental illness. The proudest time for me was when she spoke to practically a hundred psychia-

trists, doctors and mental health workers on how she was dealing with mental illness and becoming part of society again.

She has become a great spokesperson for mental illness and is helping a lot of people deal with this awful disease that is still not understood. She is helping the patients, parents, care workers and hospitals.

My mother agrees – she said she can see I am truly trying to make a difference and change the stigma attached to mental illness.

It took me ten to fifteen years to truly recover, but those years taught me so much about life, and what is important in life and what is not. Those years allowed me to train my mind to know that in certain situations, I am in control and I am able to cope and manage my illness. I taught myself what to do to maintain some level of sanity throughout the day. Those years gave me the tools to figure my illness out and understand that I can live a good and decent life with a mental illness.

Sometimes people think recovery will happen in days, weeks or months. I believe you need to understand it may take years. But during those years you will learn a great deal about yourself, your mind and how to recover and live well with mental illness, maybe even in an imperfect perfect fairy tale. I truly believe it is possible.

I knew from the beginning of my illness that being open was the right thing to do. I was brought up with strong values, possibly deeper and stronger than some people have, and I always want to do the right thing in life. Being open is one hundred percent the right thing to do.

Another reason I am so open and have been for so long is that I want people to feel comfortable talking to someone who is suffering. People fear what they don't know, so if we give them knowledge, the fear may slowly disappear.

I am open because I want people to know – and to never forget – how strong they are. With or without a mental illness, you have to remember the strength you have inside you. It is there, and it will always be there. I know it because I have it and I see it in every person I meet. It is the will we all have to keep going and never give up. I believe we are built to handle the difficulties of life. It may not seem like that in the worst of times, but we are built strong. I want you to never, ever give up. Promise yourself, in this moment, that no matter what you face, you will never give up. I need everyone to know that they have the strength inside to overcome anything this world delivers.

I speak so openly because maybe by doing so I can help someone who is suffering. I speak openly to share my story, but also to hear your story. I want to listen to you and help you if you are struggling. Maybe I can help someone suffering in silence or maybe I can just for a moment let them know they are not alone.

Life will be hard. It will be hard maybe even most of the time. Just remember you are built to make it through. And I one hundred percent believe that you can recover.

Even though I sometimes get asked whether I care what people will think, I still love the question because I feel like it has a meaningful answer, just like I love every question I am asked because every question, or its answer, has meaning.

One of my other favourite questions is when I'm going to get married or whether I've found someone.

I have been asked this for years. I laugh every time someone says this to me.

My sisters stopped asking the question a very long time ago because they began to realize that you do not have to be in a relationship to be complete and happy. No one in my family asks me that question anymore because they know I am fine and happy the way I am. I am not saying I am against being in a relationship, I am just saying that maybe finding yourself and loving yourself is more important than loving someone else or having a relationship.

I feel like that concept – honestly and wholeheartedly loving yourself before you marry – is forgotten sometimes. Our lives move so quickly that I think sometimes we forget to stop and really look at ourselves and understand who we are and who we want to be. I was able to find myself a little bit earlier than some people, and that was another gift of my illness. It made me evaluate myself, look within and try to be the best version of myself. I learned to love myself and I knew that before I committed to loving anyone else, I truly had to know and understand me. I do believe you can find yourself while in a relationship, but you have to take the time to do it and that might take time away from your relationship.

It's not just that. I've also found that just about everyone who is in a relationship tells me not to be in a relationship! They all tell me that I'm fine the way I am. And this is from people around me I truly trust. Even my parents – yes, my parents – started telling me the truth about marriage, including their marriage, a few years ago. They tell me marriage and relationships are difficult, even their own, and that they take a lot of work and a lot of compromise. Compromise is not a bad thing but you have to be willing to compromise in relationships. My parents have said to me, "If you are fine and happy the way you are, then trust us, staying single is better."

This is what most people who are in relationships tell me. Don't get me wrong, I do like to date, but getting into a serious relationship for me will take a lot of in-depth thought. I won't do it until I am one hundred percent sure they're the right person for me. I would rather wait and find my soulmate before I commit to anything serious. Finding your soulmate is not an easy task, but I do believe if you take the time and you learn a lot about yourself, you can find someone to have true, loving companionship with.

I do not understand why people feel the need to give me advice about relationships. But I just tell them, "Well, marriage is difficult and I want to make sure I find the right person." I need someone who will accept schizophrenia just like I do. My illness can be difficult sometimes and if someone cannot love everything about me, they are not the right person for me.

I find it quite funny but also sad when people ask me about marriage, to the point where I do feel empathy for them. The questions do not really bother me anymore the way they used to. I am truly happy with myself and I love myself enough to know what is good for me and what is not.

So if anyone asks you when you are getting married, ask them if they are truly happy in their marriage, and tell them to tell you the truth, not what they think society wants them to say.

Images of love and happiness are embedded in everything we see in our society. We think marriage and kids at a certain age is the norm. We are supposed to finish school, marry someone, have kids and grow old together. From the minute we are introduced to movies and television, we think we will be complete if we find our prince charming or our princess and that we will live happily ever after. But it is not that simple and not that perfect.

I hope that sharing my thoughts on relationships will make people really think about who they are going to marry and why, because you honestly need to take years to figure that out.

And I do believe if you love yourself first, your soulmates will find you. And yes, I said soulmates. In my life, I have found multiple soulmates, so I do believe you can have more than one for different times in your life. And if you believe in the power of God and the energy of the universe, the universe will help you to find true love.

But even if you do find your one and only, it still will not be simple or perfect. Relationships will never be simple or perfect, just like our lives. And even if your relationship does not survive, know that because you found yourself and learned to love yourself first, you will be okay. You will be able to live your life without someone, and you will live a pretty great life on your own.

If you are in a relationship that you know is not healthy or balanced, I believe you should get out of it, even if you believe the person is your soulmate. There are many forms of abuse in relationships and none are acceptable. So, if you are in an abusive relationship, speak to anyone, someone close, a stranger, call the police, open up to anyone you can and find support to leave the relationship.

Chapter 11.
Family, Friends and Everyone Else

I am grateful for every person I have ever met.

I have had a lot of time in my life to look inward and to learn to love myself and know how to trust myself and my choices. Looking outward, however, has been very difficult for me at times. Trusting other people is hard for me to talk about, but I'm going to talk about people now.

I have had to forgive a lot of people. I have had to forget a lot of parts of my past and I've had to move on in many relationships. But I have realized that I will never focus on the negatives in any of my relationships. Yes, I have been hurt and betrayed and yes, I have cried over failed relationships. But I have also noticed that our minds tend to pick out the negatives in life and in situations, and I think we forget about the positive aspects of many things in our lives, including our relationships. With every negative there is a positive. I have always tried to look at what my relationships have taught me and how they have made me a better person, and I have always evaluated what I could have done better in my relationships. If you cannot learn from the past, you will never grow as a person. This applies to relationships too.

My parents gave me the support and love I needed during the most difficult time in my life. They made me fight, and I mean they made me really fight for myself. They wanted me to fight at all times and in every moment. And I want everyone to understand this concept – you need to always fight for yourself, no matter what situation you are faced with.

My sisters are strong women, and they have taught me what it means to be a strong woman in a world where that is sometimes frowned upon (even if indirectly). I love my sisters' spirit. Like me, they keep fighting and they never give up. No matter what life throws at us, we use it as fuel to make our lives better.

My parents raised three very strong women and I will be forever grateful for that. My sisters and their partners have given me so much joy, especially my nieces and nephews. I don't know if they understand how much joy they have brought to my life. I do not have children of my own and maybe I never will, but someone asked me once if I've ever been in love, and I responded that yes, I have. I responded right away because I deeply love my three nieces and two nephews as if they were my own children. My nieces and nephews probably do not realize this, but I would do absolutely anything for them. And if that is not love, I don't know what is.

I feel close to some of my aunts, uncles and cousins. I have a lot of respect for each and every one of them and their partners and children. I am grateful they encourage me to speak openly about my illness. Some people would be a little ashamed or embarrassed of my story, but there has never been any negativity toward me from any of my family, only encouragement. We are a well-known family in Hamilton and I thought my family would not want me to share my story and be so open, but my family has given me nothing but support and love.

I think they understand that what I am doing – giving hope and compassion to someone who might not have those things – is the right thing to do. And I think they understand that if their children ever had a mental illness, me being open about my experience might make their kids' futures a little easier.

I have grown as close as a sister to some of my cousins, and I have some friendships and some growing friendships with others. If you are going to trust anyone, trust your family.

Friendships have been difficult for me, mostly because I have difficulty trusting people. Trust is hard for me because with my schizophrenia, I still have some paranoia. It is not as strong as it was during the worst of my illness, but sometimes feelings of paranoia creep up in my life and my relationships.

I have been able to completely trust my best friend, who I met when I was in Toronto at university. I had never had a friendship like this in my life before. I could tell her I was dating Brad Pitt and she would not tell a soul, she would not sell the story, and to me that means she truly values our friendship the way I do.

I also trust my high school friend, whom I quoted earlier. We grew apart during my illness but we have grown closer through the years. What I love about her is that we talk openly about mental health. Years after my illness, she told me that when I was going through the worst of my illness she did not know what to do. She even spoke to her parents about what to do:

> Going out with Samantha for coffee or dinner was difficult. For the next three years I only saw her during the summer breaks from university. When she did talk, I couldn't follow the stories and just sat and listened, nodding my head. Sometimes I would talk and Samantha was clearly not listening and staring into space. I would have to repeat myself many times and sometimes we just sat in silence.

> I brought a friend with me so that I didn't feel so alone. I would go home and cry. My parents would sit with me and listen and help me to laugh. I told them I couldn't do it. They told me that it was about Samantha and the only thing I could do was be there. And so that's what I did. I didn't understand fully what was happening, but I was there when the phone rang, and there at the restaurant.

My friend's thoughts helped me understand why I did not have a lot of friends during the worst of my illness: no one understood it. I don't even think I fully understood my illness.

I have another friend from high school who I reconnected with too. I always called her my cool friend; everyone loved her! I was always the nerd, the one studying, trying to ace the test. She was smart but she also talked to everyone and everyone adored her.

I also thank God for my friend from elementary school. I completely trust her as well. I am her second child's godmother. This was my first godchild. I'm not sure my friend realizes how much this meant to me, to have this connection with her and her family. We do not see each other a lot, but I completely respect her and love her and I know she has prayed for me throughout my illness.

Those four friends are my favourite people in this world, and I thank God for them every day.

I had a friend from university who now does not want anything to do with me. In her eyes I made some mistakes in our friendship, and I think she made a few mistakes too, but I made those mistakes because of my paranoia and anxiety. I do care for her greatly and pray for her every day, but she does not want to speak to me anymore. That is the hardest part of having a mental illness. Because I seem to act like everyone else, people don't realize I have a mental illness, but I do and I struggle with it every day. And sometimes my paranoia and anxiety get the best of me. I wish they did not, but they do, and that can affect the people around me. I will continue to pray for this friend and think about her often, because I truly do care about her and only want the best for her.

I am grateful every day for my relationships with my family and friends. I have had friends come and go. I have decided to focus on the positive aspects of my relationships, past and present, and this focus has given me freedom. My advice to anyone who has had difficult experiences with any relationships in their lives is that you need to forgive, forget and only focus on what the relationship taught you about yourself. And maybe even let it make you strive to be a better person and to do better in future relationships.

If you are dealing with a mental illness and don't think your family and friends will support you, pay attention to the messages of support in this book given to me by those around me. You are not alone!

Never, ever forget that. You are never alone.

My niece said, "I am so proud of you. So proud to call you my aunt and watch you touch the lives of those who need your story and support the most."

My father said, "Remember we love you unconditionally and will always have your back and we are here for you."

When I was sick, people around me did not know what to do, and that is absolutely not their fault – no one knows what to do in situations they have never been in and situations they do not understand and that have not been talked about openly. I speak about my illness for many reasons, but one main reason is that I want people to understand the unknown of mental illness and not fear it.

My eldest sister describes how afraid my family was at times:

I feel so upset saying this, but I remember saying to myself that maybe we should remove the knives from the drawers in the condo in fear that she would harm my children or herself. This was a sad time for all of us, and probably when things were at the lowest!... She is telling her story in hopes that it will provide hope and inspiration, to not only the person experiencing the illness but their parents and loved ones!

I speak openly for many reasons, which I have explained. But a big one is that I want family and friends to know what to do when their son, daughter, friend, cousin, aunt, uncle or anyone around them has a mental illness, so that maybe they will reach out to that person and talk to them because they do not fear it anymore.

The more we talk about mental illness, the less fear there will be. And then maybe people with mental illness will not be alone, people around them will know how to support the person, and maybe, just maybe, this will make it a little easier on the person with a mental illness.

My cousin said, "Thank you, Samantha, for sharing your story and being an inspiration to us all. To hear your story, to see your journey and how you have overcome every obstacle you have faced, should make anyone struggling believe there will be better days, that the light will shine again...My cousin Samantha, the warrior."

My uncle said, "The fact that you have shared this with us – your family, friends, and the world – is the greatest gift you could share with everyone."

I've also discovered that fighting this illness and speaking about it can help people who aren't even dealing with a similar situation. My niece explains: "Samantha's ability to be open and vulnerable with her community about her personal experiences inspires me every day to step into the uncomfortable and know that any struggles we experience in our lives can truly be a gift, a way to dig down deep and find out who you are and how you want to show up in this world." My father agrees: "We are all stronger because of this part of our life."

My close friend said that my blog has helped her focus on her own mental health and normalize what she feels sometimes, which in turn helps her to talk to her children about mental health.

Finally, in an abusive relationship, there are no positives. If you are in such a relationship, please talk to someone about your experiences. I talk to my counsellor about the abusive relationships I have had in the past and this is helping me continue to heal from these relationships. Talking to someone helps me and reminds me that healing and growth never end.

Chapter 12.
My Recovery:
I Will Always Be a
Work in Progress

I am amazing just the way
I am, but I am also a work
in progress. I like both.

A life with mental illness is not an easy life. But really, what life is easy? I do not think I have met one person who has a truly easy life.

Trying to navigate this world while you have a chronic mental illness is difficult and I am sure it will not get any easier as time goes by. My parents always tell me it gets worse as you get older.

According to my doctors I am in recovery, but some days it doesn't feel like I am fully recovered. I do feel my recovery most days, and most days I am managing this illness pretty well, which I am happy about.

My close friend made some observations about the beginning of my recovery:

As time went on, I had to adapt to a changing Samantha. That is not a bad thing. The medication was working and Samantha was becoming more open and honest speaking about her illness. I realized that our relationship had to change. I mourned the friendship we once had and focused on the new friendship we were developing. We lost some friends along the way, but I feel like our bond is strong and everlasting because of the openness we have about talking about mental illness.

I am able to trust that I am capable of handling my illness all on my own. I think in all this talk about mental illness, we forget to talk about and focus on recovery. That's something I did a little differently. I focused on the end. Having a mental illness is difficult, and what you are going through in the moment should be validated, but I truly believe you need to focus on the recovery. Focus on the idea that this moment will pass and you will be able to live a good and decent life even in partial recovery, just like me. It might be a seventy-five percent recovered life, but it can be pretty amazing.

Do not focus on anything except how you can make this recovery work for you. I have described what worked for me, but I believe recovery is unique. You have to find what works for you. I believe everyone has the tools to build the recovery that is unique to them. I think the key is finding those unique tools tailored to you and applying them to your life. Everyone's mental illness is different, and recovery will be different and unique to each individual.

Just don't lose sight of recovery. It may sometimes seem like it will never happen, but I believe it can if you choose to focus on how to make yourself live a good life with an illness. Figuring out recovery will not be easy, but I believe it can be done. It took many, many years for me to understand this.

Every problem has a solution. Always. Find it. The solution may be one page long, ten pages or thirty pages, but every problem, whether mathematical or in life, has a solution. I didn't say it would be an easy solution, though.

Understanding that every problem has a solution is the path to recovery. Trusting yourself to know that you are capable of solving the problem in front of you is the first step. In life and in math, I truly believe that everyone is capable of solving problems. It may take an hour or twenty years but you can do it.

I do not, however, like calling mental illness a problem. I do not like that at all, because it is not just a problem. I only compared it to mathematical problems to show that mental illness can be figured out, just like a math problem. Sometimes it would take me ten minutes to find a mathematical solution and sometimes two weeks. Just remember to trust that you are capable of figuring it out. I trusted myself and had enough confidence in myself while studying for my degrees to know that I was capable of solving these problems, so I guess in some ways I applied my math skills to my life.

Living with a mental illness is never easy. What someone with a mental illness experiences needs to be validated and acknowledged. I have learned, however, that focusing too much on the worst parts of my illness has done me no good, so years ago I chose to only focus on the good that it has brought to my life. Yes, I still have rough days, but I have learned to manage them and I believe everyone can learn to manage.

It's not something I want to talk about, but I have always thought the system was built for some people to fail. My theory that we can all recover is accurate, but the system isn't built that way, it's built for failure. How do we change the system? I haven't figured that out yet but I am working on it. My goal is that no one with a mental illness will ever be forgotten. Right now people are lost and forgotten in the system. I want every single person to recover and to know that they can recover. All that I am trying to convey is that I believe everyone can recover and I want you to believe it too.

I focus on recovery. That is why I continue to try to heal from my past experiences. I have a counsellor, and she is amazing. I had done a bit of work but I wasn't ready until now to put in all the work needed to heal from my past. I know healing is easier said than done. To heal, you need to talk about what happened to you.

I always want to be better. I want to improve my recovery, so I have continued to work on myself. I am and always will be a work in progress. Yes, my recovery is successful and I absolutely love my life but I will always continue to be better and improve my life.

I still have triggers from my past that I need to figure out. The mind is very interesting – it reminds you of things you think you have forgotten. The mind also reminds you there are things you cannot remember.

I have forgiven, but the mind does not forget, so I plan to work through some of my triggers to truly move on. And forgiveness is easier said than done too. You can't just wipe things from your mind sometimes.

I also have to learn to forgive myself for my past mistakes. My anxiety and paranoia sometimes make me overthink things, and I am sometimes too hard on myself about simple things. Maybe I will be able to forgive myself one day, but it might be many, many years away.

I still have more to write about my recovery. I am a work in progress. But here's a look at my life today:

In 2016 my father and I moved into a building, and with me as his partner and executive manager we operate and run our family office with a few other employees.

My father said, "What can I say, I am so proud of what you have become, what you have been through and now where you are planning to go, how you plan to help so many other people, parents and others understand mental illness, since there is still a lot of work to be done...I am proud of where you are as my daughter and partner at work."

My mom says I'm an extremely hard worker and very organized, and that "We are blessed that she is recovering from her illness, and we pray that her path forward is much easier. Whatever happens I know she is resilient and will conquer whatever challenges life brings. I am blessed to have her as my daughter and my best friend."

My eldest sister said,

Flash forward to today, and it makes me so happy to see Samantha recovering. Her sporty nature and athleticism are back and this has helped her a lot in her recovery. I'm so thankful that Samantha and I have the time now to spend together. She is probably one of my closest friends. We are very different, but I have a great love for her! She has a great heart and I think, not to be boastful, that we have the same heart! We truly like to give to others, bring joy and see people thrive and win! We also love to run races together. She does the ten kilometre and I do the five kilometre and we finish at the end, usually at the same time, LOL! We also golf together and she is an amazing golfer...

Samantha is also a great aunt to my three children. She connects with them frequently, not only on their birthdays. She is a big part of their lives and my children love her. Samantha is also the best gift-giver in our family. She always finds the perfect gift that is specific to the person. This goes back to her loving heart!

My sister's husband notes, "For many years now, Samantha has been well. She has her quirks and fears, like we all do, but she is fully functioning. She works, she drives, she is brilliant, she has lived alone, she has run marathons."

My cousin told me it makes her super proud to see how far I've come.

It brings me so much joy to know that I am an example for others, not only in my recovery but also in my life. I will never stop growing and learning. I know I have a lot left to do and I still have a lot to learn in my life, but I am open to the possibilities of being better and living a life that everyone around me, whether family, friend or someone I don't even know, is proud of.

Chapter 13.
What I Have Learned, and What I Would Do Differently

I would do many things differently and yet nothing differently.

Learn from it – that's what I've always thought. Life gives you these amazing gifts; you need to learn from them and become better. Take a step back and try to see the world with a different viewpoint and maybe think of ways that your past has given you lessons.

I have learned many things from my illness, and I continue to learn each and every day about life, about myself and about this world. I will never stop learning because I want to be the best version of me, a person the universe would be proud of. I keep trying to learn because I strive to always be better.

So here is what I have learned through my experience with mental illness.

I have learned about life, I learned how I want to act and how I want to treat people. I learned that the best way to live is with empathy and compassion, love and joy, and kindness and generosity.

I learned that I will never make fun of another human being. I will never talk down to another person or treat another badly or in a negative way. (And don't get me wrong, I have days when I get mad at people – I can become so angry at people in my life at times. But I have learned to step back from any situation and try to learn from my faults and become better and understand that next time I become angry I need to step back and rethink how I react.)

I learned about the person I want to be, and the person I should be.

I learned that I do not need a lot of money or power to be a good and decent person.

I learned that my experience with mental illness can bring hope to people who may otherwise not have hope.

I learned that people look at you and look up to you every day, so the best way to live is by example.

I learned about the relationships that matter most to me and I learned about loving myself first.

I learned to trust myself.

I learned that I do not need to be married or in love to be fulfilled. I learned that I am enough.

I learned how to be independent.

I learned that there is a solution to every problem, even if it seems like there isn't.

I learned that I absolutely love running and fitness and health and I learned that with a little workout, my whole viewpoint on life will change.

I learned about the importance of health over money and I learned that if you do not have health, all the money in the world will not matter.

I learned that my decision to become a vegetarian at seventeen might have been the best decision for my health.

I learned that in this world there are many opinions and all are valid, even if they are not my opinions. I learned to understand other opinions and respect them, as long as they are within the law and respectful.

I learned about unconditional love from my parents, my nieces and nephews, and God.

I learned the strength of God and spirituality in my life and I learned that God does exist in innumerable ways.

I learned that love comes in so many shapes and forms.

I learned that at any moment your entire life could be taken away from you in an instant, so cherish every single day.

I learned to live a full life every single day in the best way I know how.

I learned that everyone lives their life differently and that's okay.

I learned that in everything negative there is something positive.

I learned that if I can bring a little positivity to anyone, that is what matters to me.

I learned that being non-judgemental is the most amazing way to live.

I learned to treat everyone with respect, even if they do not deserve any respect at all.

I learned that kindness matters and to be kind at all times. This world can be awful at times and we don't need to make it any worse for anyone.

I learned that everything in this world is connected.

I learned about perspective and that being open to seeing things from different perspectives is a great way to live your life.

I learned that there are many different forms of intelligence in this world, and that intelligence is subjective.

I learned that I absolutely love life and love this world, and I learned that there can be beauty in this world, even in the most broken people.

I learned about human compassion and I learned that we as humans are capable of so much more in life than we think we are.

I learned that life will always be hard, and I learned that even though life is hard, everyone has the strength and power inside them to get through the most difficult times.

I learned that life can be amazing if you take the time to really look at your life and the world around you, and I learned that life will not always be fair but as long as you take the hard times as lessons, you have done what you were supposed to do on this earth.

I learned that this world can be amazing sometimes and awful other times and oddly, sometimes both amazing and awful at the same time.

I have learned that the most broken people sometimes have the most amazing stories and that even the most broken souls can be saved.

I learned that every single person matters in this world. You matter just like I matter.

I learned that I will never stop striving to be the best person I can be.

I have learned that I want to make God proud of me, that I want God to know I have tried my best to leave this world just a little better by my being here.

I am sure I have learned many more lessons in my thirty-nine years on this earth. I know that is not the longest life, but I have been through a lot in that time.

I have promised God that I will continue to learn each and every day for the rest of my life. I will learn from the universe and take in all the lessons I can until the day I take my last breath.

Having learned all this, who would not want to tell their younger self what they should do differently or do better in their lives? I would tell my younger self so many things – about life, about decisions and about choices. When talking to people about my mental health, I always bring up what I would have done differently and what would have made my recovery a little quicker.

If I could tell my younger, mentally ill self anything, the first thing would be to run. Sign up for
a race! I would tell my younger mentally ill self to
trust me – running will change your life completely. If I had started earlier it would have sped
up my recovery.

I would tell my younger self to take your time;
do not rush into anything. You have eighty years
to figure this out, maybe more. You don't have to
figure out your life in one year as a teenager. I
would tell my younger self that you have so much
time, that you can be and do anything; it doesn't
have to be done in two years. You have all the time
in the world. Even if you do not figure it out until
you are forty, fifty, sixty, even seventy, that is fine.
There is no race in life.

I would tell my younger self to enjoy every single day because you never know what tomorrow
will bring. I deeply know that now, and that is why
I cherish every day of my life. My life changed in
one day. I lost my entire self in one day, and I
would tell myself to just enjoy each and every moment and cherish the time you have in this world
and cherish the people around you, because you do
not know what tomorrow will bring.

I would tell my younger self that one day you
will be best friends with your parents. You might

not see it now, but you will be their biggest fans and they will be your biggest supporters. My closet friends in the world are my mom and dad, and I am forever grateful for the relationship we have built. I would tell my younger self to cherish your parents, because they are probably the only people in this world who would give up everything for you and do absolutely anything for you.

I would tell my younger self to keep the faith you have. Before my illness I had a very strong faith, but I didn't truly understand my faith until I was older. I would tell my younger self that God will be there for you no matter what, God will be in your life at all times, and if you need guidance always turn to God, because God and the universe will guide you in everything you do.

I would tell my younger self to be kind to everyone you meet, because your kindness may be the only thing someone needs at that moment.

I would tell my younger self to never make fun of anyone, to never talk badly about anyone and to always be the kind person that you have always been. I would tell my younger self that even if people are horrible to you, be kind to them. Never become them.

I would tell my younger self to trust the plan, trust that you have a specific path that you need to follow in life and trust what was set out for you. It might not be what you thought, but it might just be better and maybe more interesting. You will always end up where you should be.

I would tell my younger self to understand that life will be hard, but you will get through every obstacle you face. You have the strength to get through anything. You are stronger than you know.

My life may have turned out a little differently if I had known some of those things sooner, but I learned everything I would have told my younger self when I was older and wiser and maybe more open to understanding.

If I could tell my younger self anything, it would be to know that you will be fine, no matter what you go through or what happens, you will be absolutely and undeniably fine.

Chapter 14.
Zero Suicide

Suicide is preventable.

I understand suicide. I understand why suicide happens. I wish I didn't, of course. I wish people were able to talk openly about their mental illness and about suicide, and be able to have conversations about mental illness so that suicide did not happen. I do believe we can eliminate suicide with the suicide awareness initiatives happening all over the world. As a result of my mental health journey, I believe the best action is to follow the Zero Suicide Initiative. I believe that suicide is preventable.

I understand suicidal thoughts because I have had them. I still sometimes have them in especially difficult times even though I am in recovery. I have, however, been able to talk myself through them and have learned over the years how to understand my thoughts and manage my feelings.

Suicide is never the answer. My thoughts of suicide usually are encompassed by peace. I sometimes think, maybe if I were gone, my mind would finally be at peace. My mind would not be racing, the anxiety would be gone, and if I were with God, I would no longer be crazy and have crazy thoughts. However, I know these thoughts are not true. I know that if I were gone, I would cause more damage and pain than if I were here.

I have had times when life has been difficult, and I cry in my bed at night and I think it might just be easier if I were gone. But with years of learning how to handle my mental illness, I know suicide is not the answer. I cry and cry and cry, and then I say to myself, I know tomorrow will be better and I will make it through this stronger, healthier, better and maybe even a little wiser. And even if tomorrow is not better, I know the next day might be.

With suicide, I think about my family, about what I would be losing and what they would be losing. And then I think about God, and how God has given me these struggles for a reason, and that even though my life might be difficult in this moment, God will carry me through it, like he did before. And then I think, I need to trust God, I need to trust the universe and the plan for me, because the difficult parts of my life might be there for a reason, maybe to teach me about life, myself and my strength. God and the universe will give me struggles, but they will also protect me through those struggles. I need to trust myself and the plan for me, and I need to know the world needs me, even if sometimes I think it does not.

So I cry, and I ask God why They are doing this to me, why was today so hard, why can life be so difficult sometimes. I talk to God in those moments.

I think sometimes when we are suffering we forget our purpose in this life. We forget how valuable we are in the world, and we forget we are on this path for a reason, maybe a bigger reason than we know or can imagine. Every single person has value, and sometimes we forget that, because the days can get difficult.

If you are reading this and you are struggling, never forget that you have a purpose in this world and that today may be difficult, tomorrow may be even more difficult, but eventually those feelings and thoughts will subside, and you will feel a little bit okay.

The world is not always beautiful. It can be horrible at times. And sometimes we can get lost in the darkness. Darkness is there and sometimes we feel the darkness, but the light is always there too and we can always find that light.

Never forget your value and importance, because you are awesome, you are amazing and you matter, even if you feel broken sometimes. Your awesomeness is in there and always will be and I think you know that deep down.

You are not alone in your pain, and you are not alone in your brokenness. I have felt it, I have had those thoughts that maybe it would be better if I were gone. But it will not be better if I am gone – I know this. I also know that though one day I may be feeling horrible, the next day I could be feeling better.

If you are struggling with thoughts of suicide, stop reading this and call your emergency number. In Canada and the U.S., the number is 911.

Other options are to immediately call or tell a family member you are thinking of suicide and you need help right now. Or call a hotline – even talking to someone you do not know helps. Always ask for help.

- The **Canada Suicide Prevention Service's** suicide prevention hotline is available 24 hours a day, 365 days a year.
  - 1-833-456-4566
  - https://www.crisisservicescanada.ca/en/
  - text 45645 between 4 p.m. and midnight (ET)

- **Kids Help Phone**
  - https://kidshelpphone.ca/
  - 1-800-668-6868
  - text CONNECT to 686868

- **Crisis Text Line Canada**
  - www.crisistextline.ca
  - text HOME to 686868 (powered by Kids Help Phone)

- **Crisis Outreach and Support Team (COAST)** is available in Hamilton and Niagara, Ontario, if you or someone you know is experiencing a mental health crisis
  - 905-972-8338

- **Unsuicide** has links and descriptions of web and mobile suicide crisis services. The directory is not a crisis service and does not offer counselling. Click the links to connect to help.
  - https://unsuicide.org/

Ask for help! Trust me, it does get better and it can get easier. Asking for help and speaking openly is the first step. Asking for help is always okay. You are going to get through this. It may seem difficult in the moment but it will get better.

Chapter 15.
Life Is Tough
– Stay Strong

Stronger than you
will ever know.

I have said this before and I will say this again:
you are strong enough to handle anything that is
put upon you. You may not think you are strong
enough. You may not know you are strong enough.
People will not tell you that you are strong enough,
but I will tell you, over and over and over again:
you are strong enough to handle anything.

Never would I have thought that I could recover from paranoia and schizophrenia. Never would I have thought that I, Samantha, would recover and become better and even stronger. No one told me I was strong enough. I wish someone had! Whenever I talk to someone struggling, that is what I tell them. You can make it through this, you will make it through. Will it be easy? No. Few things in life are easy. You have to work at it. You have to put time into your recovery and into figuring your life out, but you can do it. You are strong enough to handle this.

I think sometimes we forget our strength. How powerful we were made. Did I think I was strong during my illness? No. The thought really never crossed my mind. But somewhere deep inside me, I must have known, and I must have known I was going to survive this, that I was going to beat this.

I believed I could recover. If you believe you can recover you will recover. It will not be simple. It will not be easy. You've got to fight for it. That is what I did. I learned about my strength, I discovered I was strong enough to beat this, so I fought. I put in the work and I recovered.

If you forget your strength sometimes, I will remind you. If you forget about recovery and healing, I will remind you.

I decided one day that I wanted to be the best version of me I could be. I decided I was going to work on myself, figure out my illness and figure out how to recover for me, not for anyone else.

Never stop fighting for yourself. I have never stopped fighting for me and I never will. If you cannot fight for yourself, then I will fight for you and show you that you have the strength inside to fight for yourself.

Some of my fight came from my nonna Iolanda and grandmother Maria. They were both very tough women. They struggled yet they persevered. I feel blessed to have known them and to have gained their strength and knowledge. They were quiet women but fierce. Like them, I fought, and like me, you can fight too. I believe in you and I believe you have the fight in you. I see the strength in your eyes. Never forget it.

Life can be stressful. Add having schizophrenia (and anxiety, obsessive-compulsive disorder and disordered eating) and life can get pretty interesting at times. If I have learned anything in life, it is that yes, life is hard and it probably won't get much easier. But I do believe we are built strong enough to handle the tough times.

I listen to all the advice, good or bad, that anyone can give me on my illness, my life, and pretty much anything, from young people, from old people or from anyone who honestly wants to talk to me throughout my day.

I love to talk to everyone I meet about mental illness, not just my family and friends. I talk to complete strangers working at stores, people I am standing in line with, pretty much anyone.

I sometimes think people think I'm crazy, because I love to talk to everyone I meet, and maybe bring them a bit of joy and kindness in the process.

And to be honest, I am legally crazy. And since I brought up "crazy," let me say I also love using the word crazy. Normalize it! Embrace it!

That's the word we all need to hear, isn't it? Embrace! All your beauty, all your awfulness, every single amazing thing about you – embrace it. I actually think my illness is an amazing thing about me, not an awful thing. That's how I have always seen it, as something incredible about me, not something negative.

Learning about yourself is an important part of life. If you don't get to know yourself, how will you ever get to know anyone else or be able to understand anyone else? You have got to know yourself. Even for me, who knows herself pretty well, there are still things I am learning about myself each and every day and things I want to improve upon.

I have also realized that I like myself even if others don't. I really do truly like and love myself.

We are not all going to be doctors or presidents or CEOs. But that doesn't mean our lives matter any less. And it does not mean you cannot live an amazing life.

Life is pretty cool. I see life in a very different way than most people and I will be forever grateful for that. Life can be amazing, if you let it. It won't be easy, it won't be perfect, but it can be amazing. Life made me want to be a better person. I think that's pretty awesome.

You can recover. You are capable. It is possible. Trust yourself. Make a plan for your recovery and then drill it into your life. Every problem has a solution, and I believe that every mental health experience can end in recovery, no matter what the situation. Focus on your recovery, on how you are going to manage your illness, and know that you can live a good life with a mental illness.

Feel absolutely no shame in having a mental illness. I feel no shame whatsoever, even when people make comments or say things about me. I honestly couldn't care less, because their negativity and ignorance is on them, not on me.

There have been people who have told me to be quiet, to change everything I'm doing, to be different.

And you know what I say to them, or really to myself? I think I might be louder. I like what I'm doing. I want to be different. I want change. I want a fair world. I don't want to be quiet about things that matter. I don't plan to stop.

I'll continue to learn, to grow, to listen and to strive to always, and I mean always, be better.

Embracing Schizophrenia

Acknowledgements

I would like to thank every person I have met in my life, whether they are still in my life or not. There are people who have hurt me and people who have loved and helped me along my journey and I thank every single one because every experience I have been through shaped me and made me the person I am today and the person I want to be in this world.

About the Author

Samantha Mercanti was diagnosed with schizophrenia in her early twenties. She also has anxiety disorder, obsessive-compulsive disorder and disordered eating. Samantha completed a Bachelor of Science in chemistry in 2007 and an honours Bachelor of Science in applied mathematics in 2013. Since graduation she has worked in the family business.

Since 2008 Samantha has been an advocate for people with mental illness and will continue to advocate until the time when no one with a mental illness is forgotten. She has spoken at elementary schools, high schools, colleges, universities, and many other places locally and virtually about her experience with mental illness.

Samantha has volunteered since she was a teenager at local hospitals and at charities supported by her family and friends. She is an avid runner and participated in many running races as she recovered and she loves to support charities close to her heart through these races.

Samantha is known as a very honest person who holds her values very close. Every day she tries to bring good to everyone around her and she hopes to make this world a better place for everyone.

Read Samantha's blog or contact her at SamanthaMercanti.com